PYTHON FOR BEGINNERS

A Crash Course Guide to Learn Coding and Programming With Python in 7 Days.

by

Paul Richard

© **Copyright 2020 by Paul Richard**

All rights reserved.

This document is geared towards providing exact and reliable information with regards to the topic and issue covered. The publication is sold with the idea that the publisher is not required to render accounting, officially permitted, or otherwise, qualified services. If advice is necessary, legal or professional, a practiced individual in the profession should be ordered.

From a Declaration of Principles which was accepted and approved equally by a Committee of the American Bar Association and a Committee of Publishers and Associations.

In no way is it legal to reproduce, duplicate, or transmit any part of this document in either electronic means or in printed format. Recording of this publication is strictly prohibited and any storage of this document is not allowed unless with written permission from the publisher. All rights reserved.

The information provided herein is stated to be truthful and consistent, in that any liability, in terms of inattention or otherwise, by any usage or abuse of any policies, processes, or directions contained within is the solitary and utter responsibility of the recipient reader. Under no circumstances will any legal responsibility or blame be held against the publisher for any reparation, damages, or monetary loss due to the information herein, either directly or indirectly.

Respective authors own all copyrights not held by the publisher.

The information herein is offered for informational purposes solely, and is universal as so. The presentation of the information is without contract or any type of guarantee assurance.

The trademarks that are used are without any consent, and the publication of the trademark is without permission or backing by the trademark owner. All trademarks and brands within this book are for clarifying purposes only and are the owned by the owners themselves, not affiliated with this document.

TABLE OF CONTENTS

Introduction 1

Chapter # 1: What Is Python? — A Basic Definition 3

    Who Is Python Good For? 4

    Step By Step Instructions To Begin With Python 4

    Uses Of Python 5

    Python's Key Benefits 11

    Python Isn't A "Toy" Language 12

    Python Keeps Moving Forward 12

    Modules Vs Scripts 13

Chapter # 2: Is Python A Programming Language Or A Scripting Language? 14

    What's The Python Interpreter? 15

    Beginning The Python Interpreter 16

    How Does The Interpreter Run Python Scripts? 17

    Variables In Python 18

    Variable Assignment 18

    Variable Types In Python 19

    Object References 19

    Item Identity 20

    Variable Names 21

    Fundamental Data Types In Python 23

    Departure Sequences In Strings 25

    Applying Special Meaning To Characters 26

    Boolean Type, Boolean Context, And "Truthiness" 26

    Built-In Functions 27

    Records And Tuples In Python 28

    Python Lists 28

    Lists Are Ordered 29

Nested Lists...30

Lists Are Mutable 31

Lists Are Dynamic 32

Chapter # 3: Python Tuples 33

Characterizing And Using Tuples..33

Why Utilize A Tuple Rather Than A List?...................................34

Python String Formatting...35

Control Flow Statements 39

The If Statement...39

The While Statement 41

For-Statement...42

Iterators 43

Break Statement 44

Continue Statement 44

Else Clause On Loop Statements 45

The Pass Statement 46

The Try Statement 46

Chapter # 4: Exemption And Error Handling In Python 47

Syntax Error...48

Out Of Memory Error 49

Recursion Error..50

Indentation Error..52

Exceptions..53

Type Error..53

Zero Division Error..54

Built-In Exceptions 55

Console Intrude On Error...56

Standard Error..57

Arithmetic Error...57

Zero Division 57

Overflow Error 58

Assertion Error 58

Attribute Error 59

Import Error 60

Lookup Error 61

Key Error 61

Index Error 61

Memory Error 62

Name Error 62

Python Custom Exceptions 63

Bad Marks Of Python Exception Handling 64

Chapter # 5: Working With Modules In Python 65

The Import Statement 66

Writing Modules 67

More On Import Statements 68

Module Search Path 70

Byte Compiled Files 71

The Dir() Function 72

Characterizing Your Python Function 72

Functions In Python 73

The Importance Of Python Functions 75

Modularity 76

Namespace Separation 78

Capacity Calls And Definition 79

Argument Passing 82

Positional Arguments 82

Keyword Arguments 83

Return Statement 83

Chapter # 6: What Is A File? 85

File Paths 86

Line Endings 87

Character Encodings 88

Opening And Closing A File In Python 89

Text File Types 90

Reading And Writing Opened Files 91

Python Objects And Classes 92

Characterizing A Class In Python 92

Making An Object In Python 94

Constructors In Python 96

Inheritance 98

Strategy Overriding In Python 100

Python Type Conversion And Type Casting 101

Key Points To Remember 105

Chapter # 7: Python Dictionary 106

Making Python Dictionary 106

Getting To Elements From Dictionary 107

Changing And Adding Dictionary Elements 107

Removing Elements From Dictionary 108

Python Dictionary Comprehension 109

Advanced Python 110

Beginning With Alexa Python Development 110

The Understanding Skill Of Alexa 111

Setting Up Your Environment 112

Understanding The Alexa Skill Model 113

Review A Sample Intent 117

Making New Intents 121

Building The Skill Backend 124

Chapter # 8: Implementing An Interface In Python 126

Python Interface Overview 126

Casual Interfaces 127

Unicode And Character Encodings In Python 128

What's A Character Encoding? 129

So What Is A More Formal Meaning Of A Character Encoding? 130

The String Module 130

A Bit Of A Refresher 131

Considering Every Contingency: Other Number Systems 131

Enter Unicode 133

Unicode Versus Utf-8 134

Python 3: All-In On Unicode 135

Step By Step Instructions To Use Generators And Yield In Python. 136

Understanding The Python Yield Statement 138

Utilizing Advanced Generator Methods 139

Step By Step Instructions To Use.Send() 139

Step By Step Instructions To Use .Throw() 142

Step By Step Instructions To Use .Close() 142

Propelled Features Of Python And How To Use Them 143

Chapter # 9: Comparing Python With Other Languages 147

Java 147

Javascript 148

Perl 149

Tcl 149

Smalltalk 150

C++ 151

Basic Lisp And Scheme 151

Significant Reasons Why You Should Use Python Language 152

7 Reasons Why You Must Ruminate Writing Software Applications In Python 152

1) Clear And Maintainable Code 152

2) Multiple Programming Paradigms 153

3) Compatible With Major Platforms And Systems 153

4) Robust Standard Library 153
5) Many Open Source Frameworks And Tools 154
6) Simplify Complex Software Development.................................... 154
7) Adopt Test Driven Development... 155
Advantages And Disadvantages Of Python Programming Language
.... 156
Why Companies Prefer Python?... 156
Advantages Of Python 158
Restrictions Or Disadvantages Of Python 159
World-Class Software Companies That Use Python 161
Modern Light And Magic 161
Conclusion 166

INTRODUCTION

In case you're hoping to pivot to a profession in web or software development (consistently a sharp method to break into tech), you can't go in a wrong way by learning the basic trio of HTML, CSS, and JavaScript. But, to hang out in a crowded field of candidates, you'll, in the end, need to add extra programming languages to your toolbox.

That is the place things can get tricky because there are SO MANY coding languages out there. How might you know which ones are worth learning? No, it's not time to select a name from a cap—it's tied in with making sense of which programming language will give you the highest return on investment. And, that carries us to learning Python. We've assembled this guide on Python that begins from the very beginning, then deep plunges into 13 reasons why you ought to consider adding it to your skill list. Information is power, correct?

Dating from 1991, the Python programming language was viewed as a gap-filler, an approach to writing scripts that "mechanize the boring stuff" (as one mainstream book on learning Python put it) or to quickly model applications that will be implemented in different languages.

However, in the course of recent years, Python has risen as a first-class citizen in present software development, framework management, and information analysis. It is not, at this point a back-room utility language, however a significant power in web application creation and systems management, and a key driver of the explosion in large information analytics and machine learning.

Learning Python provides the developer with a wide assortment of career ways to look over. Python is a free and open-source programming language that is utilized in web programming, information science, artificial intelligence, and numerous logical applications. Learning Python allows the programmer to concentrate on taking care of issues, as opposed to concentrating on syntax. Its relative size and rearranged syntax gives it an edge over languages like Java and C++, yet the bounty of libraries gives it the force expected to achieve extraordinary things.

CHAPTER # 1
WHAT IS PYTHON? — A BASIC DEFINITION

Python is a universally useful coding language—which means that, in comparison to HTML, CSS, and JavaScript, it tends to be utilized for different kinds of programming and software development other than web development.

Python can be utilized for things like:

- Back end (or server-side) web and mobile application development
- Desktop application and software development
- Processing big data and performing numerical calculations
- Writing framework scripts (making directions that advise a PC framework to "do" something)

However, don't let Python's wide range alarm you. Much the same as those more familiar-sounding languages, Python is a simple to learn, sought after programming language that can exponentially build your chances of getting employed and with a good salary very quickly.

Who is Python Good For?

Python is a budding star in the programming scene for two major reasons: the large scope of tasks it can deal with, joined with the way that it's a very beginner-friendly language. Python code grammar utilizes English keywords, and that makes it simple for anybody to understand and begin with the language.

Step by step instructions to begin with Python

First of all, you should download some products to use to begin programming in Python.

In case you're using a personal computer that means two options:

- A Python interpreter
- A Python IDE

What is a Python interpreter? This is the product that reads the Python code and runs it. Installing an interpreter resembles showing your PC how to communicate in a foreign language.

The IDE in the interim is the "Coordinated Development Environment." This is the program that you will use to type your Python code into. You can save and open documents along these lines, and all on the interpreter when you need to run it. This is your interface for Python development.

When installing an interpreter, you have to conclude whether you will pick Python 2 or Python 3. Every version has advantages and disadvantages, yet Python 2 is not, at this point officially supported, making Python 3 the future-verification decision.

Uses of Python

Everyone is discussing python nowadays. Python is utilized by numerous huge brands, and it is assuming a fundamental role in the realm of data and technology. Python is utilized in a wide range of regions to create different applications. Here we will talk about the uses of Python.

1. Web Development: Python is much utilized in the development of server-side web applications. Python enables you to pick the structure you need to work with. Django and Pyramid are the popular frameworks available in Python. Container and Flask are micro-frameworks to be utilized for web development. CMS (Content Management System) Plone and Django are also there for quick web improvement. These structures have been utilized by a portion of the world's most amazing sites, for example, Spotify, Mozilla, Reddit, the Washington Post, and Yelp.

Python's standard library gives extraordinary supports to numerous Internet protocols:

- HTML and XML
- JSON
- E-mail handling.
- Easy-to-utilize socket interface.

2. Work area GUI Development: Python gives many answers to

build up a Graphical User Interface (GUI). Python is sent with a toolbox named 'tkinter' which is broadly utilized for GUI developments. By utilizing Python with tkinter, you can make GUI applications quick and simple. Some toolboxes widgets, Kivy (for multitouch applications), Qt through pyqt which are usable on a few stages are available separately.

3. Logical and Numeric Applications: Python is generally utilized in different logical and numeric applications in the whole world. It has numerous libraries and packages for the usage of numerical and statistical information. Some of them are given underneath:

- NumPy: It is the library for Python when it comes to multidimensional matrices and array alongside a heap of extraordinary numerical capacities to work on these arrays.

- SciPy: It is the tool which is allowed to use for Python. It has a variety of modules for linear algebra, signal and image processing, measurements, genetic algorithms.

- Pandas: It is a broadly utilized and famous library for information analysis. It is open source and allowed to be openly utilize. Panda library gives exceptionally incredible and adaptable information structures that make information control and examination modified and straightforward.

Aside from the above libraries, Python has APM Python, SymPy, PyGSL, FuncDesigner significant libraries for doing Scientific and Numerical work.

4. Training: Python is the best decision for students to master programming skills. It is anything but difficult to learn and utilize. Applications which work in Python have widespread use in training to make education interesting and fun.

5. Business Applications: Python is utilized to take care of business issues. Individuals are utilizing Python to construct E-business and different customized ERP frameworks. In these applications, you can make any kind of student management system, charge the board frameworks and online shopping site to offer types of assistance to your clients.

6. Sound/Video Applications: Audio and Video applications are on top nowadays. You can see a huge development in this division. Python has libraries which can be utilized to analyze audio/video content.

- LibROSA: Music and sound examination should be possible by utilizing a library known as LibROSA.

- pyAudio Analysis: This library can be utilized to play out different audio analysis. It incorporates Feature Extraction, Classification, and Segmentation.

- PyLivestream: This Python library enables you to stream to streaming websites at the same time, it tends to be finished by applying pure object-oriented Python and FFmpeg. Clients can stream to Facebook Live, YouTube Live and so forth.

7. Game Development: Gaming industry is expanding step by step. Python can be utilized for the game turn of events. There are numerous applications which use python to help games and in the development of games. All the add-ons of the Battlefield 2 game and its usefulness utilize Python. The universe of Tanks utilizes Python for some functionalities. Python gives you numerous tools and libraries for the improvement of games. Python is extensible, and you can utilize the Panda3D motor to create 3D games in Python.

8. AI: Machine learning is the utilization of Artificial Intelligence (AI). It centres on the advancement of projects that can get information and use it to learn for themselves. Python has enough AI libraries available for nothing, like pandas or scikit, which can deal with information and produce results rapidly and effectively. Every one of these libraries is available under GNU license. Here is the list of some different applications you can create utilizing AI and Python

- Voice Recognition
- Predicting Music Choices
- Face Recognition
- Product Recommendation
- Online Fraud Detection

9. Database Integration: Python underpins an assortment of the database to use in the development of your application. Python gives

you the adaptability to utilize ODBC interfaces to MySQL, Oracle, PostgreSQL, MS SQL Server, and others are allowed to download and utilize.

10. System Programming: Python has superb help for Network programming. Python gives a library which covers all the network protocols, encoding and decoding of information. System writing of computer programs in python is very basic when compared to the writing of system programs in C++. There are two degrees of system service access in Python. These are:

- Low-Level Access: Basic socket support and software engineers can utilize connection-oriented and connection-less protocols for programming.

- High-Level Access: In this application-level system protocols openly utilize high-level access given by Python libraries. These are HTTP, FTP, and so on.

11. Robotics: Programming a robot assumes a significant job when you are working with robots. Robots process sensor information and plan activities as per the PC programs. PC programs are a lot of guidelines that work on a contribution to creating an output. You can use Python language alongside the Raspberry Pi. This makes it highly relevant to robotics since you can utilize a Raspberry Pi to control a robot.

12. Web Scraping: Web Scraping is well known nowadays, and it is utilized to gather information from sites to settle on a suitable choice dependent on the collection of the information. Python

permits you to perform web scratching on sites quickly, and you can pull huge information from sites in a few seconds. Python has a collection of libraries, for example, Numpy, Matlplotlib, Pandas to fill this need. Here is the list of uses dependent on Web Scraping.

- Price Comparison: Website like Trivago, Policy Bazaar utilize Web Scraping
- Social Media: To discover the patterns on social media.
- Email Gathering: Many Companies utilize Web Scraping to gather Emails which they use in advertising and send messages for the promotion of their brands or item.
- Jobs Portal: Collect information from various sites' hands-on opening in different spaces and utilize that information in a single website.

13. Information Analytics: Python is the first choice for software engineers to do information analysis. You can ready information for analysis, perform simple statistical analysis, make helpful information perceptions, manage future patterns from information, and some more. Below is a list of some well-known libraries utilized in information analysis:

- NumPy
- SciPy
- Matplotlib
- Pandas

- Scikit
- Stats models
- Blaze

14. Scripting: Python scripts are little projects to mechanize some undertaking and make your activity easier. Python scripts are straightforward to utilize. For Example, your main responsibility is to react to the client email questions, and toward the end of the day, you need to check several emails on the specified topic. Here you can make a Python script and channel the necessary keyword, and you can tally the messages having this keyword without any problem.

15. Moral Hacking: Ethical hackers, for the most part, write various scripts and robotize any organized procedure, running from little network scans to wide area network packets. Python is appropriate for making these sorts of contents and implementing filters on the systems.

Python's key benefits

Python's success rotates around a few benefits it provides for the beginners and experts the same.

- Python is simple to learn and utilize

The quantity of features in the language itself is modest, requiring relatively little investment of time or effort to create your first projects. The Python syntax is intended to be clear and direct. This simplicity makes Python a perfect showing language, and it lets newcomers understand it quickly. Subsequently, developers spend more time considering the difficulties they're attempting to solve and less time thinking of language complexities or decoding code left by others.

- Python is broadly adopted and supported

Python is both famous and broadly utilized, as the high rankings in reviews like the Tiobe Index and the huge number of GitHub projects utilizing Python attest to. Python runs on each major working framework and stage, and most minor ones as well. Many significant libraries and API-powered services have Python ties or wrappers, letting Python interface freely with those directly or its services utilize those libraries.

Python isn't a "toy" language

Even though scripting and automation spread a huge lump of Python's utilization cases (more on that later), Python is also used to assemble professional-quality software, both as independent applications and as web services. Python may not be the fastest language, yet what it needs in speed, it makes up for in adaptability.

Python keeps moving forward

Every revision of the Python language adds valuable new features to keep the pace with current software development practices. Non-concurrent activities and coroutines, for example, are currently standard pieces of the language, making it simpler to write

Python applications that perform concurrent processing.

Modules vs Scripts

In the figure, the word script is utilized to refer to a document containing a consistent grouping of requests or a batch processing file. This is generally a basic program, put away in a plain text file.

Scripts are prepared continuously by an interpreter, which is liable for executing each order successively.

A plain book record containing Python code that is proposed to be directly executed by the client is generally called script, which is a casual term that means a vital program document.

Then again, a plain text file, which contains Python code that is intended to be imported and utilized from another Python file, is called a module.

Along these lines, the major difference between a module and a script is that modules are intended to be imported, while scripts are made to be directly executed.

In either case, the significant thing is to realize how to run the Python code you write into your modules and scripts.

CHAPTER # 2
IS PYTHON A PROGRAMMING LANGUAGE OR A SCRIPTING LANGUAGE?

Essentially, all scripting languages are viewed as programming languages. The important modification between the two is that programming languages are compiled, though scripting languages are decoded.

Scripting languages are slower than programming languages and normally sit behind them. Since they just run on a subset of the programming language, they have less access to a PC's local abilities.

Python can be known as a scripting language just as it as it is a programming language since it works both as a compiler and an interpreter. A standard Python can arrange Python code into bytecodes and then decipher it simply like Java and C+.

In any case, considering the recorded connection between the broadly useful programming language and the scripting language, it will be more proper to state that Python is a universally useful programming language which works pleasantly as a scripting language as well.

What's the Python Interpreter?

Python is a brilliant programming language that allows you to succeed in a wide variety of fields.

Python also includes a bit of programming called an interpreter. The interpreter is the program you'll have to run Python code and its contents on. The interpreter is a layer of programming that works between your program and your PC hardware to get your code running.

Contingent upon the Python implementation you use, the interpreter can be:

- A program written in C, like CPython, which is the core implementation of the language
- A program written in Java, as Jython
- A program written in Python itself, as PyPy
- A program implemented in .NET, as IronPython

Whatever structure the interpreter takes, the code you compose will consistently be controlled by this program. In this way, the first condition to be able to run Python scripts is to have the interpreter correctly installed on your framework.

The interpreter can run Python code in two different ways:

- As a module or script
- As a bit of code written into an intuitive session

Beginning the Python Interpreter

The least difficult approach to begin the interpreter is to open the terminal and then utilize the translator from the order line.

To open the command-line interpreter:

- On Windows, the order line is known as the command prompt or MS-DOS console. A faster method to get to it is to go to start menu → Run and type cmd.

- On GNU/Linux, the order line can be gotten to by a few applications like xterm, Gnome Terminal or Console.

- On MAC OS X, the system terminal is gotten to through Applications → Utilities → Terminal.

```
Shell
$ python3
Python 3.6.7 (default, Oct 22 2018, 11:32:17)
[GCC 8.2.0] on linux
Type "help", "copyright", "credits" or "license" for more information.
>>>
```

Now, you can write and run Python code as you wish, with the main downside being that when you close the interpreter, your code will be no more.

When you start to work intelligently, every statement and expression you type in is assessed and executed right away:

>>> print('Welcome to the World')

Welcome to the World!

>>> 2 + 15

17

>>> print('This is Real Python')

This is Real Python

How Does the Interpreter Run Python Scripts?

When you try to run Python scripts, a multi-step process starts. In this procedure, the interpreter will:

1. Practice the statements of your characters in a consecutive style

2. Compile the source code to a middle organization known as byte code

This byte code is a translation of the code into a lower-level language that is platform-independent. Its motivation is to advance code execution. Along these lines, whenever the interpreter runs your code, it'll sidestep this gathering step.

Carefully, this code improvement is just for modules (imported documents), not for executable scripts.

3. Ship off the code for execution

Now, something known as a Python Virtual Machine (PVM) comes without hesitation. The PVM is the engine motor of Python.

It is a cycle that emphasizes the guidelines of your bytecode to show them as coordinated.

The PVM isn't an isolated part of Python. It's simply part of the Python framework you've installed on your machine. The PVM is the last step of the Python interpreter.

Variables in Python

A Python variable is a held memory area to store values. A variable in a python program offers information to the PC for processing.

Each incentive in Python has a data type. Various information types in Python are Numbers, List, Tuple, Strings, Dictionary, and so on. Factors can be declared by any name or even letter sets like a, aa, abc, and so forth.

The most effective method to Declare and utilize a Variable:

Let see an example. We will declare the variable "a" and print it.

```
a=100
print (a)
```

Variable Assignment

Think about a variable as a name connected to a specific article. In Python, factors need not be declared or characterized ahead of time, similar to the case in numerous other programming languages.

To make a variable, you simply allocate a worth to it and then begin utilizing it. The task is finished with a single equals sign (=):

Variable Types in Python

In many programming languages, variables are statically written. That means a variable is at first proclaimed to have a particular information type, and the value allocated to it during its lifetime should consistently have that type.

Variables in Python are not dependent upon this limitation. In Python, a variable might be assigned a value of one kind and then re-assigned a value of a different type:

```
Python                                                              >>>
>>> var = 23.5
>>> print(var)
23.5

>>> var = "Now I'm a string"
>>> print(var)
Now I'm a string
```

Object References

What happens when you make a variable task? This is a significant question in Python because the appropriate response differs somewhat from what you'd find in numerous other programming languages.

Python is an exceptionally object-oriented language. Each thing of information in a Python program is an object of a particular type or class.

Think about this code:

>>>

>>> print(300)

300

When given the statement print(300), the mediator does the following:

- Creates a number article
- Gives it the worth 300
- Displays it to the console

Once the quantity of references to an article drops to zero, it is not, at this point available. By then, its lifetime is finished. Python will in the long run notice that it is out of reach and reclaim the allocated memory so it very well may be utilized for something different. In the PC language, this procedure is referred to as garbage collection.

Item Identity

In Python, each item that is made is given a number that uniquely identifies it. It is ensured that no two articles will have a similar identifier during any period where their lifetimes cover. When an item's reference tally drops to zero, and it is garbage gathered, as happened to the 300 articles above, its recognizing number opens up and might be utilized once more.

The built-in Python work id() restores an object's integer

identifier. Utilizing the id() work, you can check that two factors surely point to a similar item:

```python
>>> n = 300
>>> m = n
>>> id(n)
60127840
>>> id(m)
60127840

>>> m = 400
>>> id(m)
60127872
```

Variable Names

The models you have seen so far have utilized short, terse variable names like m and n. However, factor names can be more verbose. It usually is useful if they are because it makes the motivation behind the variable more apparent from the outset.

Formally, variable names in Python can be any length and can comprise also of capitalized, lowercase letters (A-Z, a-z), as well as digits (0-9), and the underscore (_). An additional limitation is that, although a variable name can contain numbers, the primary character of a variable name can't be a digit.

```python
>>> name = "Bob"
>>> Age = 54
>>> has_W2 = True
>>> print(name, Age, has_W2)
Bob 54 True
```

For instance, the entirety of coming up next are valid variable names:

Nothing can stop you from the creation of two different variables in a similar program called 'age' and 'Age,' or also 'agE.' But, it is most likely not recommended. It would certainly be likely to confuse anybody attempting to peruse your code, even you, after you'd been away from it for some time.

Every one of them are most likely better choices over n, or ncg, or something like that. In any event, you can tell from the name what the estimation of the variable is supposed to represent.

Then again, they aren't all fundamentally similarly legible. Similarly, as with numerous things, it involves personal preference, yet the vast majority would view the initial two models, where the letters are pushed together, to be more earnest to peruse, especially the one being capital in every single letter. The most regularly utilized strategies for developing a multi-word variable name are these last three examples:

- Camel Case: Second and resulting words are capitalized, to make word limits simpler to see. (Probably, it struck somebody sooner or later that the capital letters strewn all through the variable name vaguely resemble camel humps.)
- Example: numberOfCollegeGraduates
- Pascal Case: Identical to Camel Case, except the first word, is also capitalized.
- Example: NumberOfCollegeGraduates
- Snake Case: Words are isolated by underscores.

- Example: number_of_college_graduates

Fundamental Data Types in Python

Presently you realize how to associate with the Python interpreter and execute Python code. It's an ideal opportunity to dive into the Python language. First up is a discussion of the fundamental information types that are incorporated with Python.

This is what you'll realize

- You'll discover a few fundamental numeric, string, and Boolean types that are built with Python.

- You'll also get a diagram of Python's built-in functions. These are pre-written pieces of code you can call to do helpful things. You have just observed the work in print() work, yet there are numerous others.

Whole numbers

In Python 3, there is effectively no restriction to what extent a whole number worth can be. It is constrained by the amount of memory your framework has, similar to all things, however past that, a whole number can be as long as you need it to be:

```
Python                                                      >>>
>>> print(123123123123123123123123123123123123123123123 + 1)
123123123123123123123123123123123123123123124
```

Floating-Point Numbers

The float type in Python assigns a floating-point number. Float values are indicated with a decimal point. Optionally, the character e or E followed by a positive or negative whole number might be added to specify a scientific notation:

```python
>>> 4.2
4.2
>>> type(4.2)
<class 'float'>
>>> 4.
4.0
>>> .2
0.2
>>> .4e7
4000000.0
>>> type(.4e7)
<class 'float'>
>>> 4.2e-4
0.00042
```

Complex Numbers

Complex numbers are determined as <real part>+<imaginary part>j. For instance:

Example:

```
>>> 2+3j
(2+3j)
>>> type(2+3j)
<class 'complex'>
```

Strings

Strings are groupings of character information. The type of string in language Python is called str.

String literals might be delimited, utilizing either quote that are single or double. All the atmospheres between the initial delimiter and coordinating closing delimiter are a piece of the string:

Example:

```
>>> print("I am a string.")
I am a string.
>>> type("I am a string.")
<class 'str'>

>>> print('I am too.')
I am too.
>>> type('I am too.')
<class 'str'>
```

Departure Sequences in Strings

Now and then, you need Python to interpret a character or sequence of characters inside a string in an unexpected way. This may happen in one of two different ways:

- You might need to smother the first interpretation that specific characters usually are given inside a string.

- You might need to apply unique understanding to characters in a string which would ordinarily be taken literally.

You can achieve this utilizing a backslash (\) character. A backslash character in a string demonstrates that at least one of the characters that tail it ought to be dealt with extraordinarily. (This is referred to as an escape sequence because the backslash causes the subsequent character grouping to "escape" its usual meaning.)

Applying Special Meaning to Characters

Next, assume you have to make a string that contains a tab character in it. Some text editors may allow you to embed a tab character directly into your code. In any case, numerous developers think about that poor practice, for a few reasons:

- The PC can recognize a tab character and a sequence of space characters, yet you can't. To a human perusing, the code, tab and space characters are visually unclear.

- Some content tools are arranged to consequently wipe out tab characters by growing them to the proper number of spaces.

- Some Python REPL conditions won't insert tabs into code.

Boolean Type, Boolean Context, and "Truthiness"

Python 3 gives a Boolean information type. Objects of the Boolean kind may have one of two values, True or False: As you will see in up and coming instructional exercises, expressions in Python are regularly assessed in a Boolean context, which means they are interpreted to speak to truth or falsehood. A worth that is valid in the Boolean setting is now and then said to be "truthy," and one that is bogus in Boolean context is supposed to be "false."

Example:

```
>>> type(True)
<class 'bool'>
>>> type(False)
<class 'bool'>
```

Boolean items that are equivalent to True are truthy (true), and those equivalent to False are falsy (false). However, non-Boolean items can be assessed in Boolean context also and resolved to be true or false.

Built-In Functions

The Python mediator supports numerous capacities that are implicit: there were sixty-eight, as of Python 3.6. You will cover a significant number of these in the following discussions, up in setting.

Math

Function	Description
abs()	Returns absolute value of a number
divmod()	Returns quotient and remainder of integer division
max()	Returns the largest of the given arguments or items in an iterable
min()	Returns the smallest of the given arguments or items in an iterable
pow()	Raises a number to a power
round()	Rounds a floating-point value
sum()	Sums the items of an iterable

Records and Tuples in Python

Records and tuples are arguably Python's generally flexible, valuable information types. You will discover them in practically every nontrivial Python program.

Python Lists

To put it plainly, a list is a collection of arbitrary objects, to some degree much the same as an array in numerous other programming languages yet more flexible. Lists are characterized in Python by encasing a comma-separated sequence of articles in square brackets ([]), like demonstrated as follows:

Example:

>>> a = ['foo', 'bar', 'baz', 'qux']

>>> print(a)
['foo', 'bar', 'baz', 'qux']
>>> a
['foo', 'bar', 'baz', 'qux']

The significant characteristics of Python records are as per the following:

- Lists are requested.
- Lists can contain any arbitrary objects.
- List components can be gotten for the list.
- Lists can be nested to arbitrary depth.
- Lists are changeable.
- Lists are dynamic.

Every one of these features is analyzed in more detail below.

Lists Are Ordered

A rundown isn't just a collection of objects. It is an arranged collection of objects. The request wherein you determine the elements when you characterize a list is a natural attribute of that list and is kept up for that list's lifetime.

Example:

>>> a = ['foo', 'bar', 'baz', 'qux']
>>> b = ['baz', 'qux', 'bar', 'foo']
>>> a == b
False
>>> a is b
False

>>> [1, 2, 3, 4] == [4, 1, 3, 2]
False

Lists that have similar components in a different order are not the equivalent:

Nested Lists

You have seen that a component in a list can be any kind of item. That includes another list. A list can contain sublists, which thus can include sub-lists themselves, etc. to arbitrary depth.

Example:

>>> x = ['a', ['bb', ['ccc', 'ddd'], 'ee', 'ff'], 'g', ['hh', 'ii'], 'j']
>>> x
['a', ['bb', ['ccc', 'ddd'], 'ee', 'ff'], 'g', ['hh', 'ii'], 'j']

Think about this (truly thought up) example:

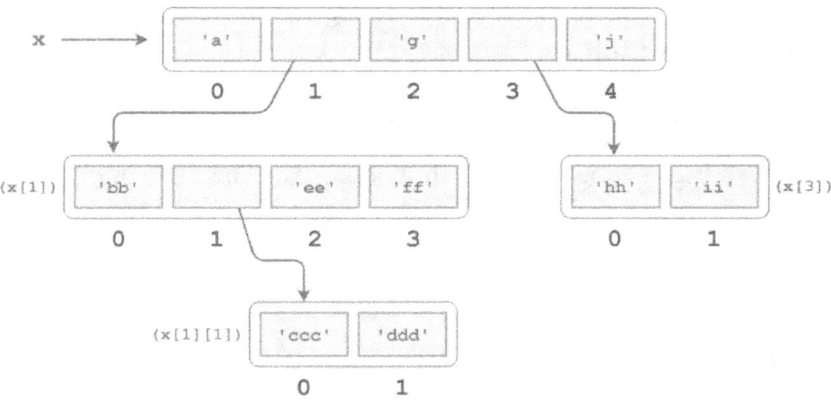

Lists Are Mutable

The more significant part of the information types you have experienced so far have been atomic types. Integer or float objects, for instance, are first units that can't be broken down. These sorts are immutable, meaning that they can't be changed once they have been assigned.

It doesn't make much sense to consider changing the value of a number. If you need a different number, you can simply assign a different one.

Conversely, the string type is a composite sort. Strings are reducible to smaller parts—the component characters. It may bode well to consider changing the characters in a string. But you can't. In Python, strings are also immutable.

The rundown is the primary mutable information type you have experienced. When a list has been made, components can be added, deleted, shifted, and moved around freely. Python gives a wide scope of approaches to modify lists.

Lists Are Dynamic

This instructional exercise started with a rundown of six characterizing attributes of Python records. The last one is that rundowns are dynamic. You have seen numerous instances of this in the segments above. Once things are added to a list, it varies:

Example:

>>> a = ['foo', 'bar', 'baz', 'qux', 'quux', 'corge']

>>> a[2:2] = [1, 2, 3]
>>> a += [3.14159]
>>> a
['foo', 'bar', 1, 2, 3, 'baz', 'qux', 'quux', 'corge', 3.14159]

CHAPTER # 3
PYTHON TUPLES

Python gives another sort that is an ordered collection of objects, called a tuple.

Pronunciation differs, depending upon whom you ask. Some pronounce it just as it was spelt "too-ple" (rhyming with "Mott the Hoople"), and others as if it were spelt "tup-ple" (rhyming with "supple"). My tendency is the last mentioned, since it probably gets from a similar cause as "quintuple," "sextuple," "octuple, etc., and everybody I know pronounces these last just as they rhymed with "supple."

Characterizing and Using Tuples

Tuples are identical to lists in all regards, except in the following properties:

- Tuples are characterized by encasing the elements in parentheses (()) rather than square brackets ([]).
- Tuples are immutable.

Here is a short model indicating a tuple definition, ordering, and slicing:

Example:

```
>>> t = ('foo', 'bar', 'baz', 'qux', 'quux', 'corge')
>>> t
('foo', 'bar', 'baz', 'qux', 'quux', 'corge')

>>> t[0]
'foo'
>>> t[-1]
'corge'
>>> t[1::2]
('bar', 'qux', 'corge')
```

Why utilize a tuple rather than a list?

- Program execution is quicker while manipulating a tuple than it is for the equivalent list.

- Sometimes you don't need the information to be adjusted. In case the values in the collection are intended to stay consistent for the life of the program, utilizing a tuple rather than a list guards against accidental modification.

- There is another Python information type that you will experience right away, called a word reference, which requires as one of its parts a worth that is of an immutable sort. A tuple can be utilized for this reason, but a list can't be.

Python String Formatting

Recall the Zen of Python and how there ought to be "one evident approach to do something in Python?" You may scratch your head when you find that there are four significant approaches to do string formatting in Python.

#1 "Old Style" String Formatting (% Operator)

Strings in Python have an exceptional, unique built-in operation that can be gotten to with the % operator. This lets you do simple positional formatting without any problem. If you've at any point worked with a printf-style work in C, you'll perceive how this works quickly. Here's a simple example:

Example:

```
>>> 'Hello, %s' % name
"Hello, Bob"
```

I'm utilizing the %s format specifier here to disclose to Python where to substitute the value of name, spoke to as a string.

There are other format specifiers available that let you control the output format. For instance, it's possible to change numbers over to hexadecimal documentation or add whitespace padding to produce pleasantly arranged tables and reports.

The "old-style" string formatting syntax changes somewhat, in case you need to make numerous replacements in a single string. Since the % operator takes just a single argument, you have to wrap the right-hand side in a tuple, as so:

Example:

\>>> 'Hey %s, there is a 0x%x error!' % (name, errno)
'Hey Bob, there is a 0xbadc0ffee error!'

This makes your format strings easier to keep up and simpler to modify in the future. You don't need to stress over creation once you ensure the request you're entering in the qualities coordinates with the request in which the values are referenced in the format string. The drawback is that this method requires somewhat more typing.

I'm certain you've been asking why this printf-style formatting which is designated "old-style" string is arranging. It was technically superseded by "new style" organizing in Python 3, which we're going to discuss here.

#2 "New Style" String Formatting (str.format)

Python 3 introduced another way of doing string designing that was also later back-ported to Python 2.7. This "new style" string formatting gets rid of the %-operator unique grammar and makes the syntax for string organizing more standard. Arranging has been presently taken care of by calling .format() on a string object.

You can utilize format() to do simple positional formatting, much the same as you could with "old style" formatting:

Example:

>>> 'Hello, {}'.format(name)
'Hello, Bob'

Or on the other hand, you can refer to your variable substitutions by name and use them in any request you need. This is a seriously amazing element as it takes into account re-arranging the request for the show without changing the arguments put into format():

Example:

>>> 'Hey {name}, there is a 0x{errno:x} error!'.format(
... name=name, errno=errno)
'Hey Bob, there is a 0xbadc0ffee error!'

This also demonstrates that the sentence structure to organize an int. variable as a hexadecimal string has changed. Presently you have to pass a format spec by including a:x suffix. The format string syntax has gotten all the more impressive without complicating, the easier to use cases.

In Python 3, this "new style" string formatting is to be favoured over %-style formatting. While "old-style" organizing has been de-emphasized, it has not been deprecated. It is as yet upheld in the most recent versions of Python. As indicated by this discussion on the Python dev email list and this issue on the Python dev bug tracker, %-formatting is going to stay for quite a while;.

#3 String Interpolation/f-Strings (Python 3.6+)

Python 3.6 included another string formatting approach called designed string literals or "f-strings". This better approach for formatting strings lets you utilize installed Python expressions inside string constants. Here's a basic guide to give you a vibe for the feature:

Example:

>>> f'Hello, {name}!'
'Hello, Bob!'

As should be obvious, this prefixes the string constant with the letter "f"— henceforth the name "f-strings." This new formatting syntax is powerful. Since you can install self-assertive Python expressions, you can even do inline arithmetic with it. Look at this model:

Example:

>>> a = 5
>>> b = 10
*>>> f'Five plus ten is {a + b} and not {2 * (a + b)}.'*
'Five plus ten is 15 and not 30.'

Control Flow Statements

A program's control stream is the request where the program's code executes. The control stream of a Python program is directed by conditional statements, loops, and function calls. This area covers the 'if' and 'for' statement and keeping in mind that loops functions are covered later in this part. Raising and taking care of exemptions also influences the control stream.

The if Statement

Regularly, you have to execute a few statements only if some condition holds, or pick explanations to execute depending on a few unrelated conditions. The Python compound statement 'if,' which utilizes if, elif, and else clauses, lets you conditionally execute blocks of statements. Here's the sentence structure for the if-statement:

Example:

if expression:
    statement(s)
elif expression:
    statement(s)
elif expression:
    statement(s)
...
else:
    statement(s)

The else-if and else clauses are optional. Note that not at all like a few languages, Python doesn't have a switch statement, so you should utilize if, else-if, and else for all conditional processing.

When there are different explanations in a clause (i.e., the condition controls a block of statements), the statements are put on independent, consistent lines after the line containing the condition's keyword (which is known as the header line of the clause) and indented rightward from the header line. The block terminates when space comes back to that of the clause header (or further left from that point). When there is only a single simple statement, as here, it can follow 'the:' on a similar sensible line as the header, however, it can also be set on a different logical line, following the header line and indented rightward from it. Numerous Python experts consider the different line style more readable:

Example:

if x < 0:
   print "x is negative"
elif x % 2:
   print "x is positive and odd"
else:
   print "x is even and non-negative"

The while Statement

The while explanation in Python supports repeated execution of a statement or block of statements that is constrained by a conditional expression. Here's the sentence structure for the while statement:

while expression:
statement(s)

Sometimes statement can also incorporate an else provision and break and proceed with statements.

Here's an average while statement:

```
count = 0
while x > 0:
    x = x // 2          # truncating division
    count += 1
print "The approximate log2 is", count
```

In the first place, expression, which is known as the circle condition, is evaluated. If the condition is bogus, the while statement ends. If the loop condition is fulfilled, the statement or statements that involve the circle body are executed. When the loop body wraps up, the loop condition is assessed once more, to check whether another loop ought to be performed. This procedure proceeds until the loop condition is false, so, all things considered, the while statement ends.

The loop body ought to contain code that eventually makes the loop condition false, or the loop will never end except if a special case is raised or the loop body executes a break statement. A loop that is in a capacity's body also closes if a return statement executes insider loop body, as the entire capacity finishes for this situation.

For-Statement

For-statement in Python helps repeated execution of an announcement or block of statements that are constrained by an iterable expression. Here's the syntax for the for-statement:

for target in iterable:
statement(s)

Note that the 'in' keyword is a piece of the syntax of the for-statement and is practically random to the in operator utilized for participation testing. A for statement can also incorporate an else provision and break and proceed with statements, as we'll examine without further ado. Iterable might be any Python expression suitable as an argument to work 'in' or work 'iter,' which restores an iterator object (clarified in detail in the following section). Target is ordinarily an identifier that names the control variable of the loop; the for-statement rebinds this variable more to everything concerning the iterator, all together. The statement or statements that include the loop body execute once for everything in iterable (except if loop ends due to an exception which occurs or if a return or break statement is performed).

Iterators

An iterator is any item I to such an extent that you can call I .next( ) with no arguments. I .next( ) restores the following thing after iterator I, or, when iterator I has no more words, it raises a StopIteration exception. When you write a class, you can allow cases of the class to be iterators by defining such a technique next. Most iterators are worked by implicit or explicit calls in work iter. Calling a generator also returns an iterator, as we'll talk about later in this section.

The for-statement implicitly calls iter to get an iterator. The following statement:

for x in c:
statement(s)

Break Statement

The break statement is allowable specifically within a loop body. When break executes, the loop ends. In case a loop is settled inside different loops, break terminates only the innermost nested loop. In viable use, a break statement is for the most part inside some clause of an if-statement on the up and up body, so it executes conditionally.

One regular utilization of break is in the execution of a loop that chooses if it should continue looping just in the centre of each loop iteration:

```
while True:            # this loop can never terminate naturally
    x = get_next( )
    y = preprocess(x)
    if not keep_looping(x, y): break
    process(x, y)
```

Continue Statement

The continue statement is allowed uniquely inside a loop body. Once proceed executes, the current iteration of the loop body ends, and execution proceeds with the next iteration of the loop. In down to earth use, a continue statement is as a rule inside some clause of an if-statement on the up and up body, so it executes conditionally.

The continue statement can be utilized instead of profoundly nested if statements inside a loop. For instance:

for x in some_container:
  if not seems_ok(x): continue
  lowbound, highbound = bounds_to_test( )
  if x<lowbound or x>=highbound: continue
  if final_check(x):
    do_processing(x)

Else Clause on Loop Statements

Both the while and for statements may alternatively have a trailing else statement. This is the announcement or statement after the else executes when the loop normally ends (toward the finish of 'for' iterator or when the while loop condition turns out to be false), however not when the loop ends rashly (using break, return, or a special case). When a loop contains at least one break explanations, you frequently need to check whether the loop ends normally or prematurely. You can utilize an else condition on the loop for this reason:

for x in some_container:
  if is_ok(x): break   # item x is satisfactory, terminate loop
else:
  print "Warning: no satisfactory item was found in container"
  x = None

The pass Statement

The body of a Python compound statement can't be unfilled—it must contain at any rate one statement. The pass statement, which plays out no activity, can be utilized as a placeholder when a statement is syntactically required; however, you don't have to do anything explicit. Here's a case of using go in a conditional statement as a piece of somewhat tangled rationale, with fundamentally exclusive conditions being tried:

```
if condition1(x):
   process1(x)
elif x>23 or condition2(x) and x<5:
   pass                    # nothing to be done in this case
elif condition3(x):
   process3(x)
else:
   process_default(x)
```

The try Statement

Python supports taking care of special cases with the try statement, which incorporates try, aside from, at last, and else statements. A program can explicitly raise an exemption with the raise statement.

CHAPTER # 4
EXEMPTION AND ERROR HANDLING IN PYTHON

Before we get into why exemption taking care of is basic and the built-in exceptions that Python underpins, it is important to understand that there is a subtle difference between a mistake and a special case.

Errors can't be dealt with, while Python special cases can be taken care of at the run time. A blunder can be a syntax (parsing) error, while there can be numerous sorts of special cases that could happen during the execution and are not unconditionally inoperable. An Error may show basic issues that a sensible application ought to make an effort not to get, while an Exception may indicate conditions that an application should try to get. Mistakes are a type of unchecked exception and are irrecoverable like an OutOfMemoryError, which a developer ought to make an effort not to deal with.

Exemption dealing with makes your code more durable and helps prevent potential failures that would make your program stop in an uncontrolled way. Suppose you have written a code which is deployed in production and still, it ends because of a special case, your customer would not welcome that, so it's smarter to deal with the specific exception already and avoid the chaos.

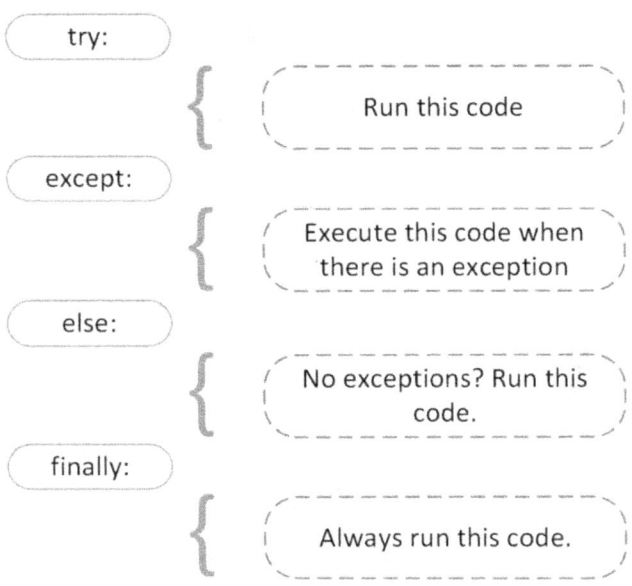

Errors can be of different kinds:

- Syntax Error
- Out of Memory Error
- Recursion Error
- Exceptions

How about we see them individually.

Syntax Error

Syntax errors frequently called parsing errors are predominantly caused when the parser detects a syntactic issue in your code.

How about we take a guide to get it.

Input:

a = 8
b = 10
c = a b

Output:

File "<ipython-input-8-3b3ffcedf995>", line 3
  c = a b
      ^

SyntaxError: invalid syntax

The up arrow demonstrated when the parser ran into a blunder or error while executing the code. The token going before the arrow causes the failure. To rectify such crucial mistakes, Python will do the greater part of your activity since it will print the document name for you and the line number at which the error occurred.

Out of Memory Error

Memory errors are, for the most part, reliant on your systems RAM and are identified with Pile. In case you have huge objects (or) referenced items in memory, at that point, you will see OutofMemoryError (Source). It tends to be caused because of different reasons:

- Using a 32-piece Python Architecture (Maximum Memory Allocation given is extremely low, between 2GB - 4GB).
- Loading a huge information document
- Running a model regarding Machine Learning and Deep Learning some more.

You can deal with the memory error with the assistance of 'special case taking care of,' a special fallback case for when the mediator completely runs short on memory and should promptly stop the current execution. In these different examples, Python raises an OutofMemoryError, allowing the script to some way or another get itself and break out of the memory error and heal.

But, since Python receives the executive engineering of the C language (malloc() work) to the memory, it isn't sure that all procedures of the script will recover — at times, a MemoryError will bring about an unrecoverable crash. Thus, neither one is decent for practicing to utilize special case dealing with for such an error, nor is it advisable.

Recursion Error

It is identified with stack and happens when you call functions. As the name recommends, recursion error transpires when an excessive number of techniques, one within other is performed (one with a boundless recursion), which is constrained by the size of the stack.

All your nearby factors and strategies call related information will be set on the stack. For every technique call, one stack edge will be made, and local, just as strategy call relevant data will be set inside that stack frame. When the technical execution is finished, the stack edge will be removed.

To repeat this error, we should characterize a function recursion that will be recursive, which means it will continue calling itself as an infinite loop technique call, you will see StackOverflow or a Recursion Error because the stack casing will be populated with method data for each call, however, it won't be freed.

def recursion():
    return recursion()

recursion()

RecursionError   Traceback (most recent call last)

<ipython-input-3-c6e0f7eb0cde> in <module>
----> 1 recursion()

<ipython-input-2-5395140f7f05> in recursion()
*   1 def recursion():*
----> 2   return recursion()

... last 1 frames repeated, from the frame below ...

<ipython-input-2-5395140f7f05> in recursion()
*   1 def recursion():*
----> 2   return recursion()

RecursionError: maximum recursion depth exceeded

Indentation Error

Indentation error is comparable in soul to the syntax error and falls under it. However, specific to the main space-related issues in the script.

So we should take a quick guide to understand an indentation error.

Input:

for i in range(10):
print('Hello world')

Output:

*File "<ipython-input-6-628f419d2da8>", line 2
    print('Hello world')
    ^
IndentationError: expected an indented block*

Exceptions

Regardless of whether the syntax of a statement or expression is right, it might even cause an error when executed. Python exceptions are errors that are recognized during execution and are not unconditionally fatal: you will learn before long in the instructional exercise how to deal with them in Python programs. An exemption object is made when a Python script raises a special case. In case the script unequivocally doesn't deal with the exception, the program will be forced to terminate abruptly.

The programs, for the most part, don't handle exceptions, and result in error messages as shown here:

Type Error

Input:

*for i in range(10):
print('Hello world')*

Output:

TypeError   Traceback (most recent call last)

<ipython-input-7-86a706a0ffdf> in <module>
    1 a = 2
    2 b = 'DataCamp'
----> 3 a + b

TypeError: unsupported operand type(s) for +: 'int' and 'str'

Zero Division Error

Input:

100 / 0

Output:

ZeroDivisionError   Traceback (most recent call last)

<ipython-input-43-e9e866a10e2a> in <module>
----> 1 100 / 0

ZeroDivisionError: division by zero

There are different sorts of Python special cases, and the sort is printed as a major aspect of the message: the sorts in the above two models are ZeroDivisionError and TypeError. Both the error strings printed as the exemption type are the name of the Python's built-in exception.

The rest of the error line gives the details of what caused the error depends on the type of exception.

How about we presently see Python's built-in exceptions.

Built-in Exceptions

```
BaseException
 +-- SystemExit
 +-- KeyboardInterrupt
 +-- GeneratorExit
 +-- Exception
      +-- StopIteration
      +-- StandardError
      |    +-- BufferError
      |    +-- ArithmeticError
      |    |    +-- FloatingPointError
      |    |    +-- OverflowError
      |    |    +-- ZeroDivisionError
      |    +-- AssertionError
      |    +-- AttributeError
      |    +-- EnvironmentError
      |    |    +-- IOError
      |    |    +-- OSError
      |    |         +-- WindowsError (Windows)
      |    |         +-- VMSError (VMS)
      |    +-- EOFError
      |    +-- ImportError
      |    +-- LookupError
      |    |    +-- IndexError
      |    |    +-- KeyError
      |    +-- MemoryError
      |    +-- NameError
      |    |    +-- UnboundLocalError
      |    +-- ReferenceError
      |    +-- RuntimeError
      |    |    +-- NotImplementedError
      |    +-- SyntaxError
      |    |    +-- IndentationError
      |    |         +-- TabError
      |    +-- SystemError
      |    +-- TypeError
      |    +-- ValueError
      |         +-- UnicodeError
      |              +-- UnicodeDecodeError
      |              +-- UnicodeEncodeError
      |              +-- UnicodeTranslateError
      +-- Warning
           +-- DeprecationWarning
           +-- PendingDeprecationWarning
           +-- RuntimeWarning
           +-- SyntaxWarning
           +-- UserWarning
           +-- FutureWarning
           +-- ImportWarning
           +-- UnicodeWarning
           +-- BytesWarning
```

Before you begin learning the built-in exceptions, we should just rapidly change the four primary segments of exemption taking care of, as appeared in this diagram.

- Try: It will run the code hinder in which you anticipate that an error to occur.

- Except: Here, you will characterize the type of exception you expect in the try block (built-in or custom).

- Else: If there isn't any exception, at that point this square of code will be executed (think about this as a cure or a fallback option if you anticipate that a piece of your script should deliver a special case).

- Finally: Irrespective of whether there is a special case or not, this square of code will consistently be executed.

Console Intrude on Error

The KeyboardInterrupt special case is raised when you attempt to stop a showing project by pressing ctrl+c or ctrl+z in an order line or interrupting on the part in Jupyter Notebook. Once in a while, you probably won't expect to interrupt a program. Yet, unintentionally, it occurs, in which case using exception handling to keep away from such issues can be useful.

In the example below, in case you run the cell and interfere with the portion, the program will raise a KeyboardInterrupt exception. inp = input(). Let's presently handle the KeyboardInterrupt exception.

```
try:
    inp = input()
    print ('Press Ctrl+C or Interrupt the Kernel:')
except KeyboardInterrupt:
    print ('Caught KeyboardInterrupt')
else:
    print ('No exception occurred')
```

Caught KeyboardInterrupt

Standard Error

We should find out about a portion of the standard errors that could generally happen while programming.

Arithmetic Error

- Zero Division Error
- OverFlow Error
- Floating Point Error

The entirety of the above special cases fall under the Arithmetic base class and are brought up for errors in arithmetic operations, as talked about here.

Zero Division

Once the divisor (second argument of the division) or the denominator is zero, the resultant raises a zero division error.

```
try:
   a = 100 / 0
   print (a)
except ZeroDivisionError:
      print ("Zero Division Exception Raised." )
else:
   print ("Success, no error!")
```

Zero Division Exception Raised.

Overflow Error

The Overflow Error is raised when the outcome of a number of juggling activity is out of range. OverflowError is raised for whole numbers that are outside a required range.

```
try:
   import math
   print(math.exp(1000))
except OverflowError:
      print ("OverFlow Exception Raised.")
else:
   print ("Success, no error!")
```

Overflow Exception Raised.

Assertion Error

Once an attested statement is failed, an Assertion Error is raised.

How about we take a guide to understand the attestation error. Suppose you have two variables a & b, which you have to look at.

```
try:
    a = 100
    b = "DataCamp"
    assert a == b
except AssertionError:
    print ("Assertion Exception Raised.")
else:
    print ("Success, no error!")
```

Assertion Exception Raised.

Attribute Error

When a non-existent attribute is referenced, and that quality reference or task comes up short, an attribute error is raised.

As you can see below, the Attributes class object has no attribute with the name attribute.

```
class Attributes(object):
    a = 2
    print (a)

try:
    object = Attributes()
    print (object.attribute)
except AttributeError:
    print ("Attribute Exception Raised.")
```

2

Trait Exception Raised.

Import Error

ImportError is raised when you attempt to import a module that doesn't exist (unable to load) in its standard way or any event when you make a grammatical mistake in the module's name. **Import nibabel**

```
ModuleNotFoundError              Traceback (most recent call last)
<ipython-input-6-9e567e3ae964> in <module>
----> 1 import nibabel

ModuleNotFoundError: No module named 'nibabel'
```

Lookup Error

Lookup Error goes about as a base class for the exceptions that happen when a key or file utilized on a mapping or sequence of a list/dictionary is invalid or doesn't exist.

The two kinds of exemptions raised are:

- IndexError
- KeyError

Key Error

If a key you are trying to get to isn't found in the word reference, a key mistake exemption is raised.

```
try:
    a = {1:'a', 2:'b', 3:'c'}
    print (a[4])
except LookupError:
    print ("Key Error Exception Raised.")
else:
    print ("Success, no error!")
```

Key Error Exception Raised.

Index Error

When you are trying to get to a file (grouping) of a list that doesn't exist in that rundown or is out of the scope of that list, an index error is raised.

```
try:
   a = ['a', 'b', 'c']
   print (a[4])
except LookupError:
   print ("Index Error Exception Raised, list index out of range")
else:
   print ("Success, no error!")
```

File Error Exception Raised, list index out of range

Memory Error

As talked about before, Memory Error is raised when an activity doesn't get enough retention to procedure added.

Name Error

Name Error is elevated when a confined or common name isn't found.

In the below example, ans variable isn't characterized. Subsequently, you will get a name error.

```
try:
   print (ans)
except NameError:
   print ("NameError: name 'ans' is not defined")
else:
   print ("Success, no error!")
```

NameError: name 'ans' isn't defined

Python Custom Exceptions

As studied in the past segment of the instructional exercise, Python has many built-in exceptions that you can use in your program. Some of the time, you may need to make custom exceptions with custom messages to fill your need.

You can achieve this by making another class, which will be gotten from the pre-characterized Exception class in Python.

```
class UnAcceptedValueError(Exception):
    def __init__(self, data):
        self.data = data
    def __str__(self):
        return repr(self.data)

Total_Marks = int(input("Enter Total Marks Scored: "))
try:
    Num_of_Sections = int(input("Enter Num of Sections: "))
    if(Num_of_Sections < 1):
        raise UnAcceptedValueError("Number of Sections can't be less than 1")
except UnAcceptedValueError as e:
    print ("Received error:", e.data)
```

Enter Total Marks Scored: 10

Enter Num of Sections: 0

Received error: Number of Sections can't be less than 1

In the above model, you saw that if you enter anything short of 1, a custom exception will be raised and dealt with. Numerous standard modules characterize their exceptions to report mistakes that may happen in functions they define.

Bad marks of Python Exception Handling

Utilizing Python exception handling has a symptom, too. Example, programs that make use attempt except squares to deal with special cases will run marginally slower, and the size of your code will increase.

The following is a model where the time it module of Python is being utilized to check the execution time of 2 unique explanations. In stmt1, the try-except form is utilized to deal with ZeroDivisionError, while in stmt2, the statement is utilized as a typical check condition. The time of execution for both of the statements is unique. You will find that stmt1, which is dealing with the exception, took a marginally longer time than stmt2, which is simply checking the worth and sitting idle if the condition isn't met.

CHAPTER # 5
WORKING WITH MODULES IN PYTHON

Modules empower you to part portions of your program in various documents for simpler support and better performance.

As a fledgeling, you begin working with Python on the interpreter; later, when you have to write longer programs, you begin writing scripts. As your program develops more in size, you might need to part it into a few records for simpler support just as reusability of the code. The answer to this is Modules. You can characterize your most utilized capacities in a module and import it, rather than duplicating their definitions into various projects. A module can be brought in by an additional program to utilize its usefulness. This is the way you can utilize the Python standard library also.

A module is a file consisting of Python code. It can define functions, classes, and factors, furthermore, can likewise incorporate runnable code. Any Python record can be referenced as a module. A document containing Python code, for instance: test.py, is known as a module, and its name would be tested.

There are different strategies for writing modules. However, the least complex path is to make a document with a .py expansion which contains capacities and factors.

Before you begin writing your modules, I suggest you investigate our Intro to Python for Data Science course, which covers the fundamentals of the Python programming language.

This instructional exercise will manage you through writing your Python modules. You will find out about the following topics:

- The import statement in Python
- Writing Modules
- More on import statements
- Module Search Path
- Byte Compiled Files
- The dir() work

The import statement

To utilize the usefulness present in any module, you need to bring it into your current program. You have to utilize the import keyword along with the ideal module name. When the translator runs over an import proclamation, it imports the module to your present program. You can utilize the capacities inside a module by utilizing a speck(.) operator along with the module name. To initiate, how about we observe how to utilize the standard library modules. In the model below, the math module is brought into the program with the goal that you can utilize sqrt() function defined in it.

For efficiency reasons, every module is just imported once per interpreter session. Thus, if you change your modules, you should restart the interpreter, if it's only one module you need to test interactively, use reload(), for instance: reload(module_name).

Writing Modules

Since you have figured out how to import a module in your program, the time has come to write your own, and use it in another program. Writing a module is much the same as writing some other Python file. We should begin by writing a function to add/subtract two numbers in a record calculation.

```
def add(x,y):
    return (x+y)
def sub(x,y):
    return (x-y)
```

In case you attempt to execute this content on the order line, nothing will happen because you have not taught the program to do anything. Make another python script in a similar index with name module_test.py and write following code into it.

```
import calculation        #Importing calculation module
print(calculation.add(1,2))  #Calling function defined in add module.
```

When the translator went over the import statement, it imported the calculation module in your code and afterwards by utilizing the dot operator, you had the option to get to the include() work.

More on Import Statements

There are more approaches to import the modules:

- from .. import statement
- from .. import * statement
- retitling the imported module

from.. import statement

The from...import statement permits you to import explicit functions/variables from a module as opposed to bringing in all things. In the past model, when you brought count into module_test.py, both the add() and sub() capacities were imported. Nevertheless, envision a situation where you just required the add() work in your code.

Here is a guide to representing the utilization of from...import

from calculation import add

the print(add(1,2))

In the above model, just the add() work is imported and utilized. Notice the utilization of include()? You would now be able to get to it directly without utilizing the module name. You can import various qualities too, isolating them by separating with a comma in the import articulation. Investigate the following model:

from count import add, sub

from .. import * statement

You can import all characteristics of a module using this statement. This will make all characteristics of the imported module noticeable in your code.

However, here is a guide to representing the utilization of from .. import *:

> *from calculation import ***
> *print(add(1,2))*
> *print(sub(3,2))*

Note that in the expert world, you ought to avoid utilizing 'from..import and from..import*,'

As it makes your code less readable.

Renaming the imported module

You can rename the module you are bringing in, which can be helpful in situations when you need to give a more meaningful name to the module or the module name is too vast even to consider using it more than once. You can utilize it as a keyword to rename it. The following example explains how to utilize it in your program.

> *import calculation as cal*
> *print(cal.add(1,2))*

You save yourself some composing time by renaming calculation as cal.

Note that you presently can't utilize calculation. Add (1,2) any longer, as the calculation is not, at this point recognized in your program.

Module Search Path

You may require your modules to be utilized in various projects/programs, and their physical area in the directory can be different. If you need to utilize a module residing in some other catalogue, you have a few options provided by Python.

When you import a module named calculation, the interpreter first searches for an implicit module with that name. If not discovered then it scans for a document named calculation.py in a rundown of registries given by the variable sys.path.

sys.path contains these areas:

- The catalogue is containing the input script (or the current registry).
- PYTHONPATH (a list of directory names, with a similar syntax as the shell variable PATH).
- The installation-dependent default.

Accept module_test.py is in the/home/datacamp/catalog, and you moved calculation.py to/home/test/. You can alter sys.path to incorporate/home/test/in the list of ways, wherein the Python interpreter will search for the module. For this, you have to alter module_test.py in the following way:

import sys
sys.path.append('/home/test/')

import calculation
print(calculation.add(1,2))

Byte Compiled Files

Bringing in a module builds the execution time of projects, so Python has a few stunts to speed it up. One route is to create byte-compiled files with the extension .pyc.

Inside, Python changes over the source code into an intermediate form called bytecode, it then interprets this into the native language of your PC and then runs it. This .pyc record is helpful whenever you import the module from a different program - it will be a lot faster since a bit of the processing required for bringing in a module is already done. Additionally, these byte-compiled files are platform-independent.

Note that these .pyc files are normally made in a similar index as the comparing .py files. If Python doesn't have permission to write to documents in that registry, then the .pyc files won't be made.

The dir() function

The dir() function is utilized to discover all the names characterized in a module. It restores a sorted list of strings containing the names defined in a module.

```
import calculation
print(test.add(1,2))
print(dir(calculation))
```

Output:
['__builtins__', '__cached__', '__doc__', '__file__', '__loader__', '__name__', '__package__', '__spec__', 'add', 'sub']

In the yield, you can see the names of the capacities you characterized in the module, include and sub. Characteristic __name__ contains the name of the module. All traits starting with an underscore are default python attributes related with a module.

Characterizing Your Python Function

All through the past instructional exercises in this series, you've seen numerous models showing the utilization of implicit Python functions.

This is what you'll realize in this instructional exercise:

- How capacities work in Python and why they're beneficial
- How to characterize and call your Python work
- Mechanisms for passing contentions to your capacity

- How to return information from your capacity back to the calling condition

Functions in Python

You might be comfortable with the mathematical concept of capacity. Capacity is a relationship or mapping between one or more inputs and a set of outputs. In arithmetic, a function is regularly spoken to like this:

$$z = f(x, y)$$

Here, f is a function that works on the data sources x and y. The output of the capacity is z. In any case, programming functions are significantly more summed up and adaptable than this mathematical definition. Suitable function definition and use are so basic to appropriate software development that all current programming languages support both implicit and user-defined functions.

In programming, capacity is an independent square of code that encapsulates a particular task or related group of tasks.

```
>>> s = 'foobar'
>>> id(s)
56313440
```

You've been introduced with a portion of the built-in functions given by Python. id(), for instance, takes one argument and returns that object's unique integer identifier: len() restores the length of the argument put into it:

```
>>> a = ['foo', 'bar', 'baz', 'qux']
>>> len(a)
4
```

Each of these built-in functions plays out a particular task. The code that achieves the task is defined somewhere, yet you don't have to know where or even how the code functions. All you have to think about is the function's interface:

1. What arguments (assuming any) it takes

2. What qualities (assuming any) it returns

At that point, you consider the capacity and pass the proper arguments. Program execution heads out to the designated body of code and does its valuable thing. Once the capacity is done, execution comes back to your code, the last known point of interest. The capacity might return information for your code to use, as the examples above do.

When you characterize your Python work, it works just the same. From someplace in your code, you'll call your Python function, and program execution will move to the variety of code that makes up the function.

Once the capacity is done, execution comes back to the area

where the capacity was called. Contingent upon how you designed the function's interface, information might be passed in when the capacity is called, and return might be passed back when it finishes.

The Importance of Python Functions

Virtually all programming languages utilized today support a type of client characterized function, even though they aren't continuously called functions. In different languages, you may see them referred to as one of the following:

- Subroutines
- Procedures
- Methods
- Subprograms

Abstraction and Reusability

Assume you think of some code that accomplishes something helpful. As you proceed with development, you find that the errand performed by that code is one you frequently need, in a wide range of areas within your application. What would be a good idea for you to do? You could simply replicate the code, again and again, utilizing your editor's copy-and-paste capability.

Later on, you'll most likely conclude that the code being referred to should be adjusted. You'll either discover some kind of problem with it that should be fixed, or you'll need to improve it here and there. If duplicates of the code are dissipated all over your application, then you'll have to make the fundamental changes in each area.

A better solution is to characterize a Python work that performs the task. Anyplace in your application that you have to achieve the task, you mostly call the capacity. Down the line, if you choose to change how it functions, at that point, you just need to change the code in one area, which is where the function is defined. The progressions will consequently be picked up anywhere the function is called.

The abstraction of functionality into a capacity definition is a case of the Don't Repeat Yourself (DRY) Principle of software development. This is arguably the most grounded inspiration for utilizing functions.

Modularity

Capacities permit complex procedures to be separated into smaller steps. Imagine for instance, that you have a program that reads in a file, forms the record substance, and then writes an output document. Your code could resemble this:

```
# Main program

# Code to read file in
<statement>
<statement>
<statement>
<statement>

# Code to process file
<statement>
<statement>
<statement>
<statement>

# Code to write file out
<statement>
<statement>
<statement>
<statement>
```

In this model, the main program is a lot of code strung together in a long grouping, with whitespace and comments to help organize it. However, if the code were to get a lot lengthier and more complex, at that point, you'd have an inexorably tough time wrapping your head around it.

Throughout everyday life, you do this kind of thing constantly, regardless of whether you don't explicitly consider it that way. If you needed to move some shelves full of stuff from one side of your garage to the next, then you ideally wouldn't only remain there and aimlessly think, "Gracious, wow. I have to move all that stuff over yonder! How would I do that???" You'd divide the activity into manageable steps:

1. Take all the stuff off the shelves.
2. Separated the shelves.
3. Carry the shelf parts over the carport to the new area.
4. Re-arrange the shelves.
5. Carry the stuff over the garage.
6. Put the stuff back on the shelves.

Breaking a large task into littler, bite-sized sub-tasks helps make the huge errand simpler to consider and manage. As projects become more complicated, it is better to modularize them like this.

Namespace Separation

A namespace is an area of a program wherein identifiers have meaning. As you'll see beneath, when a Python work is called, another namespace is made for that work, one that is particular from all different namespaces that as of now exist.

The practical upshot of these factors can be characterized and utilized inside a Python work regardless of whether they have the same name as variables characterized in different capacities or principle programs. In these cases, there will be no interface since they're kept in separate namespaces.

This means when you compose code within a function, you can utilize variable names and identifiers without worrying over whether they're being utilized somewhere else outside the capacity. This helps minimize errors in code extensively.

Capacity Calls and Definition

The usual syntax for characterizing a Python work is as follows:

def <function_name>([<parameters>]):

<statement(s)>

The last thing, <statement(s)>, is known as the body of the capacity. The body is a square of statements that will be executed when the capacity is called. The body of a Python work is characterized by space as per the off-side guideline. This is equivalent to code blocks related to a control structure, similar to the if or while statement.

The syntax for calling a Python work is as per the following:

<function_name>([<arguments>])

<arguments> are the qualities gone into the function. They relate to the <parameters> in the Python work definition. You can characterize a function that doesn't take any arguments. However, the brackets are as yet required. Both a capacity definition and a capacity call should consistently incorporate parentheses, regardless

of whether they're empty.

Of course, you'll start with a little model and include complexity from that point. Remembering the time-honoured mathematical tradition in mind, you'll call your first Python work f(). Here's a script file, foo.py, that characterizes and calls f():

```
def f():
    s = '-- Inside f()'
    print(s)

print('Before calling f()')
f()
print('After calling f()'
```

Here's how this code works:

1. Line 1 uses the def keyword to demonstrate that capacity is being defined. Execution of the def statement only makes the meaning of f(). All the accompanying lines that are indented (lines 2 to 3) become some portion of the group of f() and are put away as its definition, yet they aren't executed at this point.

2. Line 4 is a touch of whitespace between the function definition and the first line of the main program. While it isn't syntactically necessary, it is ideal to have. To become familiar with whitespace around top-level Python work definitions, look at

Writing Beautiful Pythonic Code with PEP 8.

3. Line 5 is the main statement that isn't indented because it is anything but a piece of the meaning of f(). It's the beginning of the fundamental program. When the fundamental program executes, this statement is executed first.

4. Line 6 is a call to f(). Note that empty parentheses are required continuously in both a function definition and a capacity call, in any event, when there are no boundaries or contentions. Execution continues to f(), and the statements in the variety of f() are executed.

5. Line 7 is the following line to execute once the assemblage of f() has ended. Execution comes back to this print() statement.

The sequence of execution (or control stream) for foo.py appears in the following diagram:

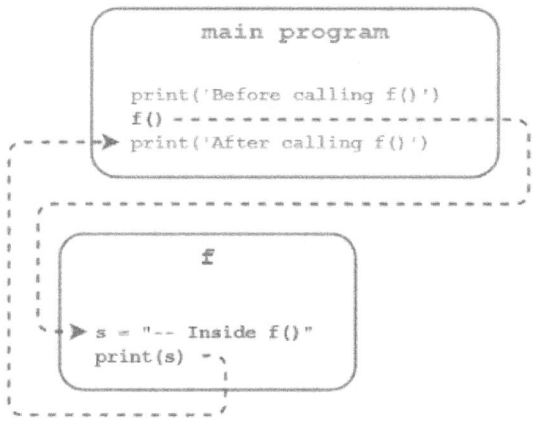

Argument Passing

So far, in this instructional exercise, the functions you've defined haven't taken any arguments. This can now and then be helpful, and you'll occasionally write this kind of functions. All the more frequently, however, you'll need to pass information into capacity with the goal that its behaviour can shift starting with one invocation then onto the next. How about we see how to do that.

Positional Arguments

The most direct approach to pass arguments to a Python function is with positional arguments (additionally called required arguments). In the function definition, you indicate a comma-separated list of boundaries inside the parentheses:

```
>>> def f(qty, item, price):
...     print(f'{qty} {item} cost ${price:.2f}')
...
```

In some programming writings, the parameters given in the capacity definition are referred to as formal parameters, and the arguments in the capacity call are referred to as actual parameters:

```
        Function Call                Function Definition
    f(6, 'bananas', 1.74)    →    def f(qty, item, price):
          arguments                       parameters
       (actual parameters)            (formal parameters)
```

Keyword Arguments

When you're calling a function, you can determine arguments in the form <keyword>=<value>. Each <keyword> must match a boundary in the Python work definition. For instance, the recently characterized function f() might be called with keyword arguments as follows:

```
>>> f(qty=6, item='bananas', price=1.74)
6 bananas cost $1.74
```

Return Statement

What's a Python capacity at this point? All things considered, as a rule, if a function doesn't cause some adjustment in the calling condition, then there isn't a lot of point in calling it by any means. By what method should a function affect its caller?

Indeed, one chance is to utilize function return values. A return statement in a Python work fills two needs:

1. It promptly ends the function and passes execution control back to the guest.

2. It gives an instrument by which the capacity can pass information back to the caller.

Reading and Writing Files in Python

One of the most widely recognized tasks that you can do with Python is reading and writing files. Regardless of whether its simple text file, reading a complicated server log, or in any event, examining raw byte data, these circumstances require reading or writing a document.

CHAPTER # 6
WHAT IS A FILE?

Before we can go into how to function with documents in Python, it's essential to understand what precisely a record is and how present-day working systems handle a portion of their aspects.

At its centre, a file is a contiguous arrangement of bytes used to store information. This information is sorted out in a particular organization, what's more, can be anything as basic as a text document or as an executable program. At long last, these byte files are then converted into binary 1 and 0 for simpler processing by the computer.

Files on most present-day file systems are made out of three major parts:

1. Header: metadata about the substance of the record (document name, size, type, etc.)

2. Data: the substance of the record as written by the maker or creator or editor

3. End of file (EOF): an exceptional character that demonstrates the finish of the file

What this information speaks to relies upon the format specification used, which is normally spoken to by an extension. For instance, a record that has an extension of .gif probably fits in with the Graphics Interchange Format detail. There are hundreds, if not thousands, of record extensions out there. For this instructional exercise, you'll just arrange with .txt or .csv record extensions.

File Paths

When you get to a file on a working system, a record way is required. This documented way is a string that speaks to the area of a file. It's split up into three significant parts:

1. Path of the folder: the record folder area on the document framework where ensuing organizers are isolated by a forward cut/(Unix) or backslash \ (Windows)

2. File Name: the genuine name of the document

3. Extension: the finish of the document way pre-pended with a period (.) used to demonstrate the file type

Here's a quick example. Suppose you have a document situated inside a file structure this way:

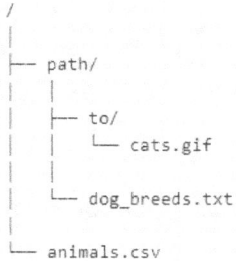

If you needed to get to the cats.gif file, and your present location was in a similar folder as away. To get to the file, you have to go to

the path of the folder and then to the organizer, at last finding the cats.gif file. The Folder Path will be way/to/. The FileName is cats. The

File Extension is .gif. So the full way is way/to/cats.gif.

Presently suppose that your current location or current working directory (cwd) is in the organizer of our sample folder structure. Rather than finding to the cats.gif by the full way of way/to/cats.gif, the file can be just referenced by the file name and extension 'cats.gif.'

Line Endings

One issue regularly experienced when working with extension information is the representation of another line or line finishing. The line finishing has its underlying foundations from back in the Morse code period when a particular pro-sign was utilized for communicating the finish of a transmission or the finish of a line.

Afterwards, this was normalized for teleprinters by both the International Organization for Standardization (ISO) and the American Standards Association (ASA). The ISO standard considered either the CR+LF characters or simply the LF character.

Windows utilizes the CR+LF characters to demonstrate another line, while UNIX and the more current Mac versions utilize only the LF character. This can cause a few complications when you're processing files on a working framework that is not the same as the file's source. Here's a quick example. Let's look at the file dog_breeds.txt that was made on a Windows framework:

```
Pug\r\n
Jack Russell Terrier\r\n
English Springer Spaniel\r\n
German Shepherd\r\n
Staffordshire Bull Terrier\r\n
Cavalier King Charles Spaniel\r\n
Golden Retriever\r\n
West Highland White Terrier\r\n
Boxer\r\n
Border Terrier\r\n
```

Character Encodings

Another basic issue that you may confront is the encoding of the byte information. Encoding is an interpretation from byte information to distinct characters. This is normally done by assigning a numerical value to speak to a character. The two most regular encodings are the ASCII and UNICODE Formats. ASCII can just store 128 characters, while Unicode can contain up to 1,114,112 characters.

ASCII is a subset of Unicode (UTF-8), implying that ASCII and Unicode share the equivalent numerical to character values. It's crucial to take note that parsing a file with the mistaken character encoding can prompt failures or deception of the character. For instance, if a file was made utilizing the UTF-8 encoding, and you attempt to parse it utilizing the ASCII encoding, if there is a character that is outside of those 128 values, at that point an error will be thrown.

Opening and Closing a File in Python

When you need to work with a file, the first thing is to open it. This is finished by invoking the open() worked in work. Open () has a required contention that is the route to the record. open() has a single return, the record object:

- record = open('dog_breeds.txt')

After you open a file or document, the next thing to learn is how to close it.

Remember that you must close the file. No matter the endless supply of an application or script, a document will be shut in the end. Nonetheless, there is no assurance when precisely, that will occur. This can lead to unwanted behaviour, including asset spills. It's also a best practice inside Python (Pythonic) ensures that your code carries on in a manner that is all around characterized and reduces any unwanted behaviour.

When you're manipulating a file, there are two different ways that you can use to guarantee that a document or file is closed appropriately, in any event, while experiencing an error. The primary method to close a record is to utilize the try-finally block:

```
reader = open('dog_breeds.txt')
try:
    # Further file processing goes here
finally:
    reader.close()
```

The next method to close a record is to utilize with the statement:

```
with open('dog_breeds.txt') as reader:
    # Further file processing goes here
```

There are three unique categories of file objects:

- Text files
- Buffered paired files
- Raw paired files

Every one of these document types is characterized in the io module. Here's a fast once-over of how everything lines up.

Text File Types

A book file is the most widely recognized record that you'll experience. Here are a few instances of how these documents are opened:

```
1  open('abc.txt')
2
3  open('abc.txt', 'r')
4
5  open('abc.txt', 'w')
```

With these sorts of files, open() will restore a TextIOWrapper file object:

```
1  >>> file = open('dog_breeds.txt')
2  >>> type(file)
3  <class '_io.TextIOWrapper'>
4
5
```

Reading and Writing Opened Files

When you've opened up a file, you'll need to read or keep in touch with the file. For one thing, how about we spread reading a file. Different techniques can be approached with a file article to help you out:

Method	What It Does
.read(size=-1)	This reads from the file based on the number of size bytes. If no argument is passed or None or -1 is passed, then the entire file is read.
.readline(size=-1)	This reads at most size number of characters from the line. This continues to the end of the line and then wraps back around. If no argument is passed or None or -1 is passed, then the entire line (or rest of the line) is read.
.readlines()	This reads the remaining lines from the file object and returns them as a list.

Python Objects and Classes

Python is an article situated programming language. Not at all like technique arranged programming, where the main emphasis is on capacities, object situated programming stresses on objects.

An item is just a collection of data (variables) and strategies (works) that follow up on that data. Also, a class is an outline for that object.

We can consider the class like a sketch (prototype) of a house. It contains all the insights concerning the floors, doors, windows and so on. Given these descriptions, we assemble the house. House is the item.

The greatest number of houses can be produced using a house's blueprint; we can make numerous items from a class. An object is also called an example of a class, and the way toward making this item is called instantiation.

Characterizing a Class in Python

Like capacity definitions start with the def keyword in Python, class definitions start with a class keyword.

The first string inside the class is called doc-string and has a brief description of the class. In spite of the fact that this is not mandatory, it is highly recommended.

Here is a simple class definition.

```python
class MyNewClass:
    '''This is a docstring. I have created a new class'''
    pass

```

A class makes new local namespace where every one of its traits is characterized. Attributes might be information or functions.

There are also unique attributes in it that start with double underscores __. For instance, __doc__ gives us the doc-string of that class.

When we characterize a class, another class object is made with a similar name. This class object allows us to get to the various ascribes to start up new objects of that class.

```python
class Person:
    "This is a person class"
    age = 10

    def greet(self):
        print('Hello')


# Output: 10
print(Person.age)

# Output: <function Person.greet>
print(Person.greet)

# Output: 'This is my second class'
print(Person.__doc__)
```

Output

```
10
<function Person.greet at 0x7fc78c6e8160>
This is a person class
```

Making an Object in Python

We saw that the class item could be utilized to get to various attributes.

It can also be utilized to make new object instances (instantiation) of that class. The technique to make an article is like a capacity call.

>>> harry = Person()

This will make another item case named harry. We can get to the attributes of items by the use of the objects named as a prefix.

Attributes might be information or method. Strategies for an article are comparing functions of that class.

Stating this way, since Person.greet is a function object (quality of class), Person.greet will be a method object.

```python
class Person:
    "This is a person class"
    age = 10

    def greet(self):
        print('Hello')


# create a new object of Person class
harry = Person()

# Output: <function Person.greet>
print(Person.greet)

# Output: <bound method Person.greet of <__main__.Person object>>
print(harry.greet)

# Calling object's greet() method
# Output: Hello
harry.greet()
```

Output

```
<function Person.greet at 0x7fd288e4e160>
<bound method Person.greet of <__main__.Person object at 0x7fd288e9fa30>>
Hello
```

You may have seen the self-parameter in function definition inside the class; however, we basically called the technique harry.greet() with no arguments. Despite that, everything worked.

The item itself is passed as the main argument. Thus, harry.greet() translates into Person.greet(harry).

When all is said in done, calling a method with a list of n arguments is comparable to calling the relating capacity with an argument list that is made by embedding's the method's object before the first argument.

Consequently, the main argument of the function in class must be simply the article. This is expectedly called self. It very well may be so named in any case, however we highly recommend to follow the show.

Presently you should be familiar with class object, occasion object, work object, technique object and their differences.

Constructors in Python

Class works that start with double underscore __ are called unique functions as they have special meaning.

Of one specific interest is the __init__ () work. This exceptional function gets called at whatever point another object of that class is started up.

This kind of function is also called constructors in Object-Oriented Programming (OOP). We ordinarily use it to instate all the factors.

```python
class ComplexNumber:
    def __init__(self, r=0, i=0):
        self.real = r
        self.imag = i

    def get_data(self):
        print(f'{self.real}+{self.imag}j')


# Create a new ComplexNumber object
num1 = ComplexNumber(2, 3)

# Call get_data() method
# Output: 2+3j
num1.get_data()

# Create another ComplexNumber object
# and create a new attribute 'attr'
num2 = ComplexNumber(5)
num2.attr = 10

# Output: (5, 0, 10)
print((num2.real, num2.imag, num2.attr))

# but c1 object doesn't have attribute 'attr'
# AttributeError: 'ComplexNumber' object has no attribute 'attr'
print(num1.attr)
```

Output

```
2+3j
(5, 0, 10)
Traceback (most recent call last):
  File "<string>", line 27, in <module>
    print(num1.attr)
AttributeError: 'ComplexNumber' object has no attribute 'attr'
```

In the above model, we characterized another class to speak to complex numbers. It has two functions, __init__ () to instate the factors (defaults to zero) and get_data() to show the number appropriately.

An interesting thing to note with regards to the above step is that attributes of an article can be made on the fly. We made another attribute attr for object num2 and read it too. In any case, this doesn't make that quality for object num1.

Inheritance

Every object-oriented programming language would not be qualified to take a look at or use if it wasn't to support inheritance. Inheritance was designed in 1969 for Simula. Python not only supports inheritance but also different inheritance too. As a rule, legacy is the system of getting new classes from existing ones. By doing this, we get a chain of importance of classes. In many class-based object-oriented languages, an item made through legacy (a "child object") gets all, - however, there are exceptions in some programming languages, - of the properties and practices of the parent object.

Inheritance allows programmers to make classes that are based after existing classes, and this makes it conceivable that a class made through inheritance inherits the characteristics and strategies for the parent class. This means that inheritance supports code reusability. The methods or as a rule, the product acquired by a subclass is viewed as reused in the subclass. The relationships of articles or classes through inheritance give rise to a directed graph.

The class from which a class inherits is known as the parent or superclass. A class which acquires from a superclass is known as a subclass, also called heir class or child class. Superclasses are in some cases called ancestors too. There exists a chain of command relationship between classes. It's like relationships or classifications that we know from reality. Consider vehicles, for instance. Bicycles, vehicles, transports and trucks are vehicles. Pick-ups, vans, sports vehicles, convertibles and home vehicles are for the most part cars, and by being cars, they are vehicles also. We could execute a car class in Python, which may have techniques like accelerating and brake. Vehicles, Busses and Trucks and Bikes can be implemented as subclasses which will acquire these techniques from the vehicle.

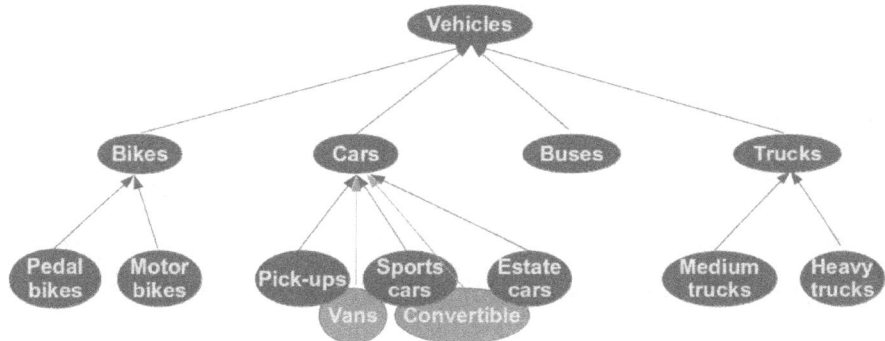

Python Inheritance Syntax

```
class BaseClass:
    Body of base class

class DerivedClass(BaseClass):
    Body of derived class
```

Derived class acquires features from the base class where new features can be added to it—this results in re-usability of use of code.

Case of Inheritance in Python

To show the utilization of inheritance, let us take an example.

A polygon is a shut figure with at least 3 sides. State, we have a class called Polygon characterized as follows.

```
class Polygon:
    def __init__(self, no_of_sides):
        self.n = no_of_sides
        self.sides = [0 for i in range(no_of_sides)]

    def inputSides(self):
        self.sides = [float(input("Enter side "+str(i+1)+" : ")) for i in range(self.n)]

    def dispSides(self):
        for i in range(self.n):
            print("Side",i+1,"is",self.sides[i])
```

This class has information attributes to store the quantity of sides n and magnitude of each side as a list called sides.

Strategy Overriding in Python

In the above model, notice that __init__() strategy was characterized in the two classes, Triangle and also Polygon. When this occurs, the method in the determined class overrides that in the base class. This is to state, __init__() in Triangle gets preference over the __init__ in Polygon.

For the most part, while overriding a base technique, we will, in general, expand the definition instead of just replace it. The same is being finished by calling the strategy in a base class from the one in a derived class (calling Polygon.__init__() from __init__() in Triangle).

A better option is to utilize the worked in work super(). In this way, super().__init__(3) is equivalent to Polygon.__init__(self,3) and is liked. To become familiar with the super() work in Python, visit Python super() work.

Two built-in functions, isinstance() and issubclass() are utilized to check inheritances.

The function instance() returns True if the article is an example of the class or different classes gotten from it. Every single class in Python inherits from the base class object.

```
1  >>> isinstance(t,Triangle)
2  True
3
4  >>> isinstance(t,Polygon)
5  True
6
7  >>> isinstance(t,int)
8  False
9
10 >>> isinstance(t,object)
11 True
12
```

Python Type Conversion and Type Casting

Type Conversion

The way toward changing over the value of one information type (whole number, string, float, and so on.) to another information type is called type conversion. Python has two sorts of type conversion.

1. Implicit Type Conversion

2. Explicit Type Conversion

Implicit Type Conversion

In Implicit type, Python naturally changes over one information type to another data type. This procedure needn't bother with any client involvement.

How about we see a model where Python promotes the conversion of the lower data type (whole number) to the higher data type (float) to stay away from data loss.

Example 1: Converting the whole number to float

```
num_int = 123
num_flo = 1.23

num_new = num_int + num_flo

print("datatype of num_int:",type(num_int))
print("datatype of num_flo:",type(num_flo))

print("Value of num_new:",num_new)
print("datatype of num_new:",type(num_new))
```

When we run the above program, the output will be:

```
datatype of num_int: <class 'int'>
datatype of num_flo: <class 'float'>

Value of num_new: 124.23
datatype of num_new: <class 'float'>
```

In the above program,

- We include two variables num_int and num_flo, putting away the value in num_new.

- We will take a look at the information kind of every one of the three objects respectively.

- In the yield, we can see that the information sort of num_int is a whole number while the information kind of num_flo is known as the float.

- Also, we can perceive that the num_new has a float information type since Python consistently changes over smaller information types to more significant information types to stay away from the loss of information.

- Example 2: Addition of string(higher) information type and integer(lower) datatype

```
1  num_int = 123
2  num_str = "456"
3
4  print("Data type of num_int:",type(num_int))
5  print("Data type of num_str:",type(num_str))
6
7  print(num_int+num_str)
8
```

Once we run the above program, the output will be:

```
Data type of num_int: <class 'int'>
Data type of num_str: <class 'str'>

Traceback (most recent call last):
    File "python", line 7, in <module>
TypeError: unsupported operand type(s) for +: 'int' and 'str'
```

Explicit Type Conversion

In Explicit Type Conversion, clients convert the information sort of an article to the required information type. We utilize the predefined functions like int(), glide(), str(), and so forth to perform explicit type conversion.

This type of transformation is also called typecasting because the client throws (changes) the data type of the objects.

Syntax:

<required_datatype>(expression)

Typecasting should be possible by doling out the necessary data type capacity to the expression.

Example 3: Addition of string and number utilizing an explicit conversion

```
num_int = 123
num_str = "456"

print("Data type of num_int:",type(num_int))
print("Data type of num_str before Type Casting:",type(num_str))

num_str = int(num_str)
print("Data type of num_str after Type Casting:",type(num_str))

num_sum = num_int + num_str

print("Sum of num_int and num_str:",num_sum)
print("Data type of the sum:",type(num_sum))
```

When we run the above program, the output will be:

```
Data type of num_int: <class 'int'>
Data type of num_str before Type Casting: <class 'str'>

Data type of num_str after Type Casting: <class 'int'>

Sum of num_int and num_str: 579
Data type of the sum: <class 'int'>
```

In the above program,

- We include num_str and num_int variable.
- We changed over num_str from string(higher) to integer(lower) type utilizing int() function to perform the addition.

- After changing over num_str to a whole number worth, Python can include these two variables.

- We got the num_sum worth and data type to be an integer.

Key Points to Remember

1. Type Conversion is the change of article starting with one information type then onto the next data type.

2. Implicit Type Conversion is naturally performed by the Python interpreter.

3. Python keeps away from the loss of information in Implicit Type Conversion.

4. Unequivocal(Explicit) Type Conversion is also called Type Casting; the information type of items are changed over utilizing predefined functions by the client.

5. In Type Casting, loss of information may happen as we implement the item to a particular data type.

CHAPTER # 7
PYTHON DICTIONARY

Python word reference is an unordered collection of things. Everything of a word reference has a key/value pair.

Word references are enhanced to retrieve values when the key is known.

Making Python Dictionary

Making a word reference is as simple as setting things inside curly braces {} separated by commas.

A thing has a key and relating esteem that is expressed as a couple (key: value).

```
# empty dictionary
my_dict = {}

# dictionary with integer keys
my_dict = {1: 'apple', 2: 'ball'}

# dictionary with mixed keys
my_dict = {'name': 'John', 1: [2, 4, 3]}

# using dict()
my_dict = dict({1:'apple', 2:'ball'})

# from sequence having each item as a pair
my_dict = dict([(1,'apple'), (2,'ball')])
```

As should be obvious from above, we can also make a word reference utilizing the built-in dict() work.

Getting to Elements from Dictionary

While ordering is utilized with other information types to access values, a word reference utilizes keys. Keys can be utilized either inside square brackets [] or with the get() technique.

If we utilize the square brackets [], KeyError is brought up if a key isn't found in the word reference. Then again, the get() strategy returns None if the key isn't found.

```
1  # get vs [] for retrieving elements
2  my_dict = {'name': 'Jack', 'age': 26}
3
4  # Output: Jack
5  print(my_dict['name'])
6
7  # Output: 26
8  print(my_dict.get('age'))
9
10 # Trying to access keys which doesn't exist throws error
11 # Output None
12 print(my_dict.get('address'))
13
14 # KeyError
15 print(my_dict['address'])
16
```

Output

```
Jack
26
None
Traceback (most recent call last):
  File "<string>", line 15, in <module>
    print(my_dict['address'])
KeyError: 'address'
```

Changing and Adding Dictionary elements

Word references are mutable. We can include new things or change the value of existing things utilizing an assignment operator.

If the key is now present then the current worth gets updated. If the key is absent, another (key: value) pair is added to the dictionary.

```
1  # Changing and adding Dictionary Elements
2  my_dict = {'name': 'Jack', 'age': 26}
3
4  # update value
5  my_dict['age'] = 27
6
7  #Output: {'age': 27, 'name': 'Jack'}
8  print(my_dict)
9
10 # add item
11 my_dict['address'] = 'Downtown'
12
13 # Output: {'address': 'Downtown', 'age': 27, 'name': 'Jack'}
14 print(my_dict)
15
```

Output

{'name': 'Jack', 'age': 27}
{'name': 'Jack', 'age': 27, 'address': 'Downtown'}

Removing elements from Dictionary

We can expel a specific thing in a word reference by utilizing the pop() method. This technique expels a thing with the given key and returns the value.

The pop item() technique can be utilized to expel and return an arbitrary (key, value) thing pair from the word reference. All the things can be removed without a moment's delay, utilizing the clear() method.

We can also utilize the del keyword to expel singular things or the entire dictionary itself.

```python
# Removing elements from a dictionary

# create a dictionary
squares = {1: 1, 2: 4, 3: 9, 4: 16, 5: 25}

# remove a particular item, returns its value
# Output: 16
print(squares.pop(4))

# Output: {1: 1, 2: 4, 3: 9, 5: 25}
print(squares)

# remove an arbitrary item, return (key,value)
# Output: (5, 25)
print(squares.popitem())

# Output: {1: 1, 2: 4, 3: 9}
print(squares)

# remove all items
squares.clear()

# Output: {}
print(squares)

# delete the dictionary itself
del squares

# Throws Error
print(squares)
```

Output

```
16
{1: 1, 2: 4, 3: 9, 5: 25}
(5, 25)
{1: 1, 2: 4, 3: 9}
{}
Traceback (most recent call last):
  File "<string>", line 30, in <module>
    print(squares)
NameError: name 'squares' is not defined
```

Python Dictionary Comprehension

Dictionary comprehension is an elegant and concise approach to make another word reference from an iterable in Python.

Word reference appreciation comprises of an expression pair (key: esteem) trailed by an explanation inside curly braces {}.

Here is a guide to making a word reference with everything being a couple of a number and its square.

109

```
1  # Dictionary Comprehension
2  squares = {x: x*x for x in range(6)}
3
4  print(squares)
5
```

Output

{0: 0, 1: 1, 2: 4, 3: 9, 4: 16, 5: 25}

Advanced Python

Turning into a Python master requires some time, yet after some time you'll ace this excellent programming language. It's justified, despite all the trouble!

Development on Alexa Python: Build and Deploy an Alexa Skill

Keen home speakers were an original thought only a few years back. Today, they've become a focal piece of numerous individuals' homes, and workplaces and their reception is just expected to grow. Among the most well-known of these devices are those controlled by Amazon Alexa. In this instructional exercise, you'll become an Alexa Python engineer by conveying your own Alexa expertise, an application that clients will communicate with utilizing voice orders to Amazon Alexa devices.

Beginning With Alexa Python Development

To follow this instructional exercise, you'll have to make a free Alexa developer account. On that page, you'll make the following steps:

1. Click the Get Started button.
2. Click Create your Amazon account.
3. Fill out the structure with the required details.
4. Click Submit to finish the sign-up process.

You'll also be familiar with ideas, for example, lists and word references in Python, just as JavaScript Object Notation (JSON). In case you're new to JSON, look at Working with JSON Data in Python.

We should begin!

The understanding skill of Alexa

The developer of an Alexa Python must be familiar with various Alexa aptitude segments, but the two most significant components are the interface and the service:

1. The skill interface forms the client's discourse sources of info and maps it to a plan.

2. The skill administration contains all the business logic that decides the reaction for given client info furthermore, returns it as a JSON object.

The expertise interface will be the frontend of your Alexa ability. This is the place you'll characterize the purposes and the invocation phrases that will play out a specific capacity. This is the piece of the ability that is answerable for associating with the clients.

The expertise service will be the backend of your Alexa ability. When a particular goal is triggered by the client, it will send that data as a demand to the expert service. This will contain the business rationale to be returned alongside significant data to the frontend, which will finally be relayed back to the client.

Setting Up Your Environment

It's an ideal opportunity to begin building your first Alexa Python skill! Sign in to the Alexa designer console and click on the Create Skill catch to begin. On the following page, enter the Skill name, which will be Joke Bot:

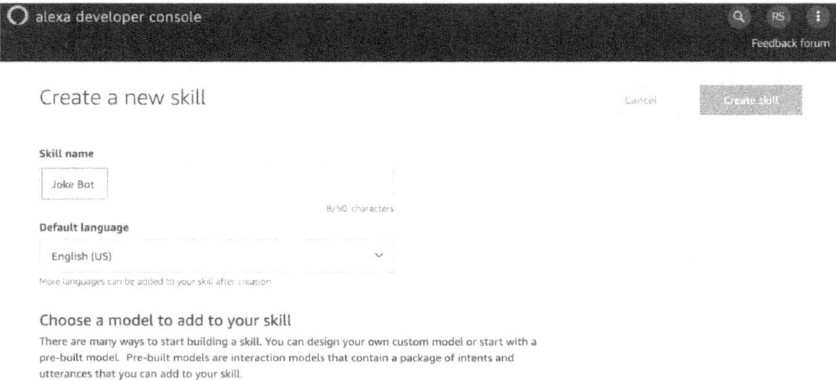

This will be the summon expression of your expertise. It's the expression a client will address to begin utilizing your Alexa skill. You can change this to something different later on if you'd like. Also, note that Alexa skills can collaborate in numerous languages, which you can see from the Default Language dropdown menu. Until further notice, simply set it to English (US).

Next, you'll have to pick a model to add to your skill. These models resemble layouts that have been pre-structured by the Amazon group to assist you with beginning with Alexa Python improvement, given some regular use cases. For this instructional exercise, you should choose the Custom model.

At last, you have to choose a technique to have the backend of your Alexa expertise. This administration will contain the business rationale of your application.

For the present, select Alexa-Hosted (Python) as the backend for your Alexa skill. This will naturally furnish you with a facilitated backend inside the AWS free tier, so you don't need to pay anything forthright or set up a complicated backend presently.

At last, click the Create Skill catch to continue. You may be approached to round out a CAPTCHA here, so complete that too. Following a moment or something like that, you ought to be diverted to the Build area of the developer console.

Understanding the Alexa Skill Model

When you've signed into the Alexa developer console and chosen or made a skill, you'll be welcomed with the Build segment. This section provides you with a lot of choices and controls to set up the association model of the ability. The parts of this interaction model allow you to characterize how the clients will interface with your expertise. These properties can be gotten to through the left-side board, which looks something like this:

113

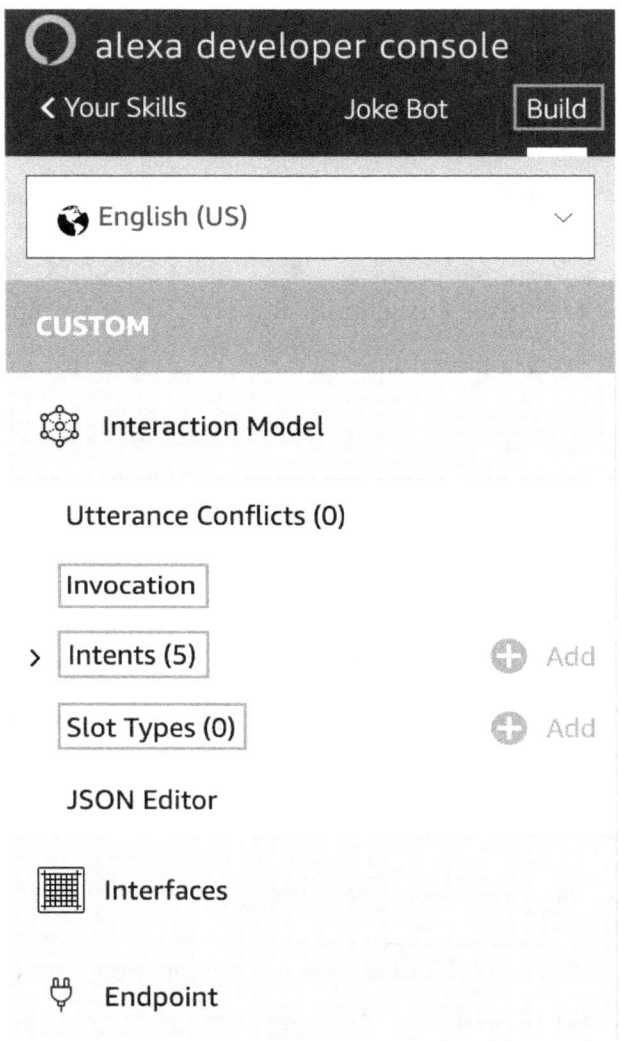

As a developer of Alexa Python, there are a couple of components of an Alexa expertise interaction model that you'll have to think about. The first is the invocation. This is the thing that clients will say to start interacting with your Alexa skill. For instance, the client will say, "Joke Bot," to invoke the Alexa skill you'll work in this instructional exercise.

Another part is the purpose, which speaks to the centre functionality of your application. Your application will have a set of intents that will speak to what types of activities your expertise can perform. To give relevant data to a given goal, you'll utilize a space, which is a variable in an utterance phrase.

Think about the following model. A sample utterance to conjure the climate aim could be, "Educate me regarding the climate." To make the skill more helpful, you can set the plan to be, "Inform me concerning the climate in Chicago," where "Chicago" will be passed as a space variable, which improves the client experience.

In conclusion, there are slot types, which define how information in space is dealt with and recognized—for instance, AMAZON.DATE space type effectively changes over words that demonstrate a date — like "today, "tomorrow", and others—into a standard date format, (for example, "2019-07-05"). You can look at the official space type reference page to find out additional slots.

Now, the Intents panel should be open. If it's not, then you can open it by choosing Intents from the sidebar on the left. You'll see that there are five purposes previously set up of course:

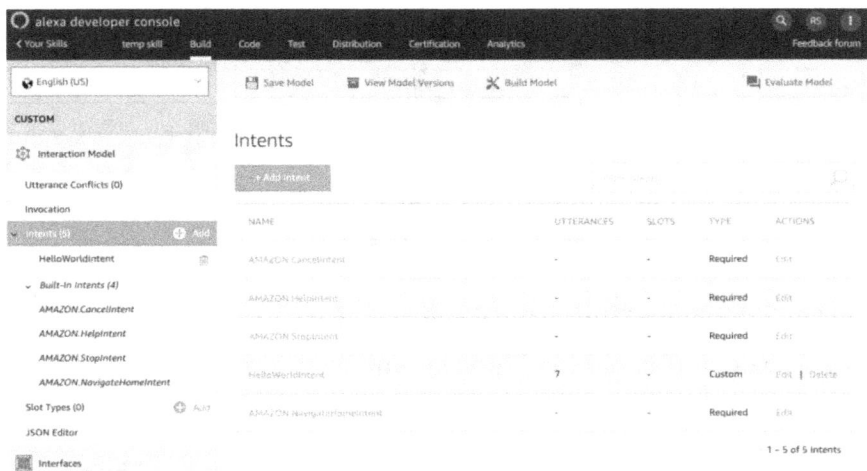

The Intents board incorporates a HelloWorldIntent and five Built-in Intents. The inherent aims are there to remind you to represent some normal cases that are essential to making an easy to use bot. Here's a brief overview:

1. AMAZON.CancelIntent lets the client drop an exchange or task. Models incorporate, "Don't bother," "Overlook it," "Exit," and "Drop," however, there are others.

2. AMAZON.HelpIntent assists on how to utilize the expertise. This could be utilized to restore a sentence that fills in as a manual for the client on the most proficient method to cooperate with your skill.

3. AMAZON.StopIntent allows the client to leave the ability.

4. AMAZON.NavigateHomeIntent navigates the client to the device home screen (if a screen is being utilized) and closes the skill session.

Of course, there are no sample utterances assigned to trigger these aims, so you'll need to include those also. Think of it as a component of your preparation as an Alexa Python developer.

Review a Sample Intent

Later in this instructional exercise, you'll figure out how to make another plan, yet until further notice, it's a smart thought to investigate some current goals that are a piece of each new skill you make. To begin, click the HelloWorldIntent to see its properties:

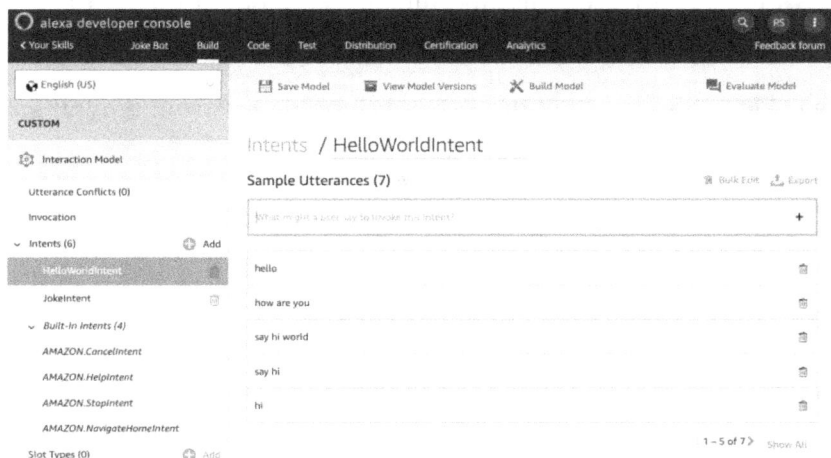

You can see the example utterances that a client can say to invoke this intent. When this goal is invoked, this data is sent to the backend service of your Alexa skill, which will, at that point, execute the necessary business logic and return a response.

Beneath this, you have the choice to set up the Dialog Delegation Strategy, which permits you to assign a particular dialog that you characterize to a specific intent.

Next, you have the option to characterize slots for some specific information that your plan should gather. For instance, if you somehow happened to make an intent that tells the whether for a given day, at that point you'd have a Date space here that would gather the date data and send it to your backend administration.

At whatever point you make changes to a purpose, you have to tap the Save Model catch to spare it. Then, you can tap the Build Model catch to feel free to test your Alexa Python skill.

It's useful to realize that the interaction model of a skill can be spoken to in a JSON position. To look at the present structure of your Alexa ability, click the JSON Editor choice from the left side panel of the console:

If you roll out a change directly using the JSON editor, the progressions are also reflected in the developer console UI. To test this conduct, include another expectation and click Save Model.

When you've made all the fundamental changes to the cooperation model of your skill, you can open the Test area of the developer console to try out your skill. Testing is a significant part of turning into an Alexa Python developer, so be certain not to avoid this progression! Snap the Test button from the top route bar on the developer console. As a matter of course, testing will be disabled. Starting from the drop menu, select Development to begin testing:

Here, you have various ways that you can try out your Alexa Python skill. How about we do a quick test with the goal that you can get an idea of how your Alexa ability will react to an expression.

Select the Alexa Simulator alternative from the left sideboard, at that point, enter the expression, "Hello Alexa, open Joke Bot." By typing it in the information box or by utilizing the Mic option. After two or three seconds, a reaction will be returned to you:

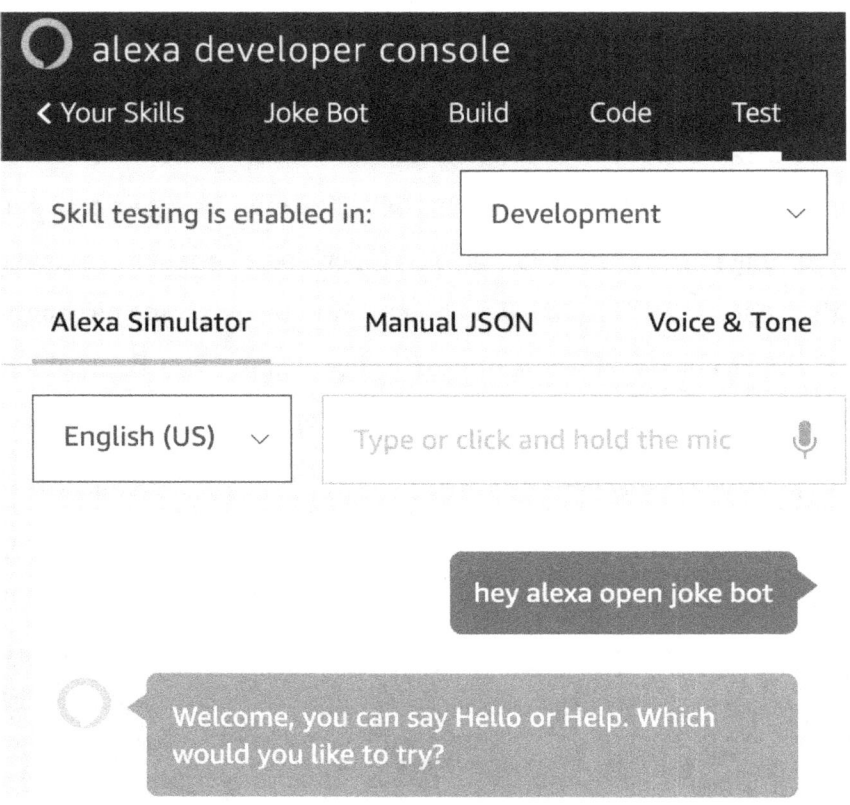

Also with the voice response, you can also observe the JSON Input that was sent to the backend service of your Alexa expertise, just like the JSON Output that was gotten back to the console:

This is what's happened up until this point:

- The JSON input object was developed from input information that the client entered through voice or text.

- The Alexa test system packaged up the contribution alongside other applicable metadata and sent it to the backend administration. You can see this in the JSON Input box.

- The backend administration got the info JSON object and parsed it to check the kind of request. Then, it passed the JSON to the relevant intent handler function.

- The purpose handler function prepared the input and gathered the necessary response, which is sent back as a JSON reaction to the Alexa test system. You can see this in the JSON Output box.

Since you have a review of the various segments of an Alexa expertise and how data streams starting with one segment then onto the next, it's an ideal opportunity to begin building your Joke Bot! In the following section, you'll put your Alexa Python developer skills to the test by making another goal.

Making New Intents

How about we start by making the JokeIntent, which will restore a random joke from a rundown to the client. At that point, click the Add button close to the Intents alternative from the left sideboard:

Interaction Model

Utterance Conflicts (0)

Invocation

∨ **Intents (5)**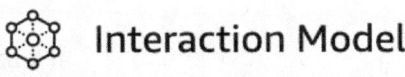

HelloWorldIntent 🗑

∨ ***Built-In Intents (4)***

With the Create custom plan choice chosen, set the name to JokeIntent and afterwards click the Create custom purpose button:

Add Intent
An intent represents an action that fulfills a user's spoken request. Learn more about intents.

○ Create custom intent

JokeIntent | Create custom intent

Next, you have to include test utterances that the client will address to invoke this goal. These can be phrases like "Make me a quip" or "I need to hear a joke." Type in the expression and click the in addition to signing (+) to include it as a sample utterance. This is what that should resemble: You can include more sample utterance, yet for the time being, these will do fine. Ultimately, click the Save Model catch in the upper left corner of the window to save these changes.

Intents / JokeIntent

Sample Utterances (2) Bulk Edit Export

| What might a user say to invoke this intent? | + |

| I want to hear a joke | 🗑 |
| Tell me a joke | 🗑 |

1 – 2 of 2

Keep in mind; you'll have to build your model before you can test it out. Snap the Build Model catch to re-assemble the interaction model of your Alexa Python aptitude. You'll see a progress notification on the base right of your browser window. When the assembling process is successful, you should see another pop-up notification indicating the status of the build procedure.

You can verify whether the JokeIntent is effectively activated or not. Snap the Evaluate Model button in the upper right corner of the developer console. A little window will fly in from the side, allowing you to check what purpose will be activated by a given input utterance. Type in any of the sample utterances to ensure that the JokeIntent is being invoked successfully.

To dispose of assessing the pop-up window, click the Evaluate Model button once more.

Since you've effectively created an intent, it's time to write the Python code that will deal with this aim and return a joke as a response.

Building the Skill Backend

Since you have a plan made that can be activated by the client, you have to include functionality in the skill backend to deal with this goal and return valuable data. Open the Code area of the Alexa developer console to get started.

When you open the Code section of the developer console, you can see an online code editor with certain files previously set up for you to begin. Specifically, you'll see the following three records in the lambda sub-directory:

1. lambda_function.py: This is the principle section purpose of the backend administration. All the request information from the Alexa expectation is gotten here and should become back from this file only.

2. requirements.txt: This file contains the rundown of Python packages that are being utilized in this task. This is particularly valuable if you're deciding to set up your backend service as opposed to utilizing what's given by Amazon. To get familiar with requirements files, look at Using Requirements Files.

3. utils.py: This file contains some utility functions required for the lambda capacity to cooperate with the Amazon S3 service. It contains some example code on the most proficient method to bring information from an Amazon S3 can, which you may find useful later on. At present, this file isn't being utilized in lambda_function.py.

CHAPTER # 8
IMPLEMENTING AN INTERFACE IN PYTHON

Interfaces assume a significant job in software engineering. As designing develops, updates and changes to the code base become more difficult to manage. As a rule, you end up having classes that look fundamentally the same, yet are unrelated, which can prompt some confusion.

Python Interface Overview

At a significant level, an interface goes about as an outline for planning classes. Like classes, interfaces characterize techniques. Unlike classes, these strategies are dynamic. A theoretical technique is one that the interface simply defines. It doesn't implement the techniques. This is finished by classes, which at that point, implement the interface and give concrete significance to the interface's abstract methods.

Python's way to deal with interface design is, to some degree, different when compared with languages like Java, Go, and C++. These languages all have an interface keyword, while Python doesn't. Python further goes amiss from different languages in one other angle. It doesn't require the class that is implementing the interface to define the entirety of the interface's abstract methods.

Casual Interfaces

In specific conditions, you may not require the strict rules of a proper Python interface. Python's dynamic nature permits you to implement an informal interface. A casual Python interface is a class that characterizes methods that can be superseded, however, there's no strict enforcement.

```
class InformalParserInterface:
    def load_data_source(self, path: str, file_name: str) -> str:
        """Load in the file for extracting text."""
        pass

    def extract_text(self, full_file_name: str) -> dict:
        """Extract text from the currently loaded file."""
        pass
```

In the following model, you'll take the point of view of an information engineer who needs to extract text from different unstructured file types, as PDFs and messages. You'll make a casual interface that characterizes the strategies that will be in both the PdfParser and EmlParser solid classes:

InformalParserInterface characterizes the two methods .load_data_source() and .extract_text(). These strategies are characterized yet not implemented. The implementation will happen once you make concrete classes that acquire from InformalParserInterface.

As should be obvious, InformalParserInterface seems to be identical from a standard Python class. You depend on duck typing to advise clients that this is an interface and ought to be utilized likewise.

Given duck composing, you characterize two classes that execute the InformalParserInterface. To utilize your interface, you should make a strong class. A strong class is a subclass of the interface that gives an implementation of the interface's strategies. You'll make two strong classes to implement your interface. The first is PdfParser, which you'll use to parse the text from PDF files:

```
1  class PdfParser(InformalParserInterface):
2      """Extract text from a PDF"""
3      def load_data_source(self, path: str, file_name: str) -> str:
4          """Overrides InformalParserInterface.load_data_source()"""
5          pass
6
7      def extract_text(self, full_file_path: str) -> dict:
8          """Overrides InformalParserInterface.extract_text()"""
9          pass
10
```

Unicode and Character Encodings in Python

Dealing with character encodings in Python or some other languages can on occasion appear to be painful. Places, for example Stack Overflow, have a huge number of questions coming from confusion over exceptions like UnicodeDecodeError and UnicodeEncodeError. This instructional exercise is intended to clear the Exception of fog and shows that working with text and double information in Python 3 can be a smooth experience. Python's Unicode support is solid and strong. However, it takes some time to master.

This instructional exercise is different because it's not language-agnostic but rather deliberately Python-driven. You'll despite everything get a language-agnostic primer, however you'll then dive into illustrations in Python, with text-heavy paragraphs kept to a base. You'll perceive how to utilize ideas of character encodings in live Python code.

What's a Character Encoding?

There are tens if not several character encodings. The ideal approach to begin understanding what they are is to cover one of the least difficult character encodings, ASCII.

Regardless of whether you're self-trained or have a formal computer science background, odds are you've seen an ASCII table a few times. ASCII is a formal computer science background to begin finding out about character encoding since it is a little and contains encoding. (Excessively little, notably.)

It incorporates the following:

- Lowercase English letters: a through z

- Uppercase English letters: A through Z

- Some punctuation and images: "$" and "!", to name a couple

- Whitespace characters: a genuine space (" "), just as a newline, carriage return, level tab, vertical tab, and a couple of others

- Whitespace characters: characters, for example, delete, "\b", that can't be printed actually in the way that the letter A can

So what is a more formal meaning of a character encoding?

At an elevated level, it's a method of interpreting characters, (for example, letters, and punctuation, images, whitespace, and control characters) to numbers and eventually to pieces. Each character can be encoded to a special succession of bits. Try not to stress in case you're shaky on the idea of bits since we'll get to them in the blink of an eye.

The different classes are sketched out to speak to gatherings of characters. Every single character has a comparing code point, which you can consider as only a number. Characters are divided into various ranges within the ASCII table:

The string Module

Python's string module is a helpful one-stop-look for string constants that fall in ASCII's character set.

Here's the centre of the module in the entirety of its brilliance:

```
# From lib/python3.7/string.py

whitespace = ' \t\n\r\v\f'
ascii_lowercase = 'abcdefghijklmnopqrstuvwxyz'
ascii_uppercase = 'ABCDEFGHIJKLMNOPQRSTUVWXYZ'
ascii_letters = ascii_lowercase + ascii_uppercase
digits = '0123456789'
hexdigits = digits + 'abcdef' + 'ABCDEF'
octdigits = '01234567'
punctuation = r"""!"#$%&'()*+,-./:;<=>?@[\]^_`{|}~"""
printable = digits + ascii_letters + punctuation + whitespace
```

The majority of these constants ought to act naturally when recording in their identifier name. We'll cover what hex digits and octdigits are in a matter of seconds.

You can utilize these constants for regular string control.

A Bit of a Refresher

This is a decent and ideal opportunity for a short update on the bit, the most basic unit of information that a computer knows. A piece is a sign that has just two possible states. There are various methods of symbolically representing a piece that all mean something very similar:

- 0 or 1
- "yes" or "no."
- True or False
- "on" or "off."

Our ASCII table from the past area utilizes what you and I would simply call numbers (0 through 127), yet what are all the more precisely called numbers in base 10 (decimal). You can also communicate every one of these base-10 numbers with a grouping of bits (base 2). Here are the parallel renditions of 0 through 10 in decimal:

Considering every contingency: Other Number Systems

In the conversation of ASCII above, you saw that each character maps to a number in the variety 0 through 127.

This scope of numbers is communicated in decimal (base 10).

The way you, I, and all of us people are accustomed to tallying, for reasons unknown and more entangled than that we have 10 fingers.

However, there are other numbering systems also that are particularly prevalent all through the CPython source code. While the "hidden number" is the same, all numbering systems are simply various methods of expressing the same number.

If I asked you what number the string "11" speaks to, you'd be wholly correct to give me a weird look before noting that it speaks to eleven.

However, this string representation can communicate different underlying numbers in various numbering frameworks. However, decimal, the choices incorporate the following normal numbering frameworks:

- Binary: base 2
- Octal: base 8
- Hexadecimal (hex): base 16

However, you may not get what it means for us to state that, in a specific numbering system, numbers are spoken to in base N?

Here is the ideal way that I can explain what this means: it's the number of fingers that you'd depend on in that system.

In case you need a fuller but still gentle introduction to numbering frameworks, Charles Petzold's Code is an extraordinarily cool book that investigates the foundations of PC code in detail.

One approach to exhibit how different numbering systems interpret something very similar is with Python's int() constructor. In case you pass a str to int(), Python will expect as a matter of course that the string communicates a number in base 10 except if you reveal to it in any case:

```
>>> int('11')
11
>>> int('11', base=10)  # 10 is already default
11
>>> int('11', base=2)   # Binary
3
>>> int('11', base=8)   # Octal
9
>>> int('11', base=16)  # Hex
17
```

Enter Unicode

As you saw, the issue with ASCII is that it's not nearly a big enough set of characters to suit the world's arrangement of dialects, lingos, images, and glyphs. (It's not even large enough for English alone.)

Unicode, in a general sense, fills a similar need as ASCII. However, it just encompasses a way greater set of code points. There are a bunch of encodings that rose sequentially among ASCII and Unicode. Yet, they are not so much worth referencing right now because Unicode and one of its encoding plans, UTF-8, has gotten so predominantly used.

Consider Unicode a massive version of the ASCII table—one that has 1,114,112 possible code focuses. That is 0 through 1,114,111, or 0 through 17 * (216) - 1, or 0x10ffff hexadecimal.

Indeed, ASCII is an ideal subset of Unicode. The initial 128 characters in the Unicode table relate accurately to the ASCII characters that you'd reasonably expect them to.

In light of being technically exacting, Unicode itself isn't an encoding. Or maybe, Unicode is executed by various character encodings, which you'll see soon. Unicode is a better idea as a guide (something like a dict) or a 2-section table of the database. It maps characters (like "a", "¢", or even "﷼") to particular, positive whole numbers. A character encoding needs to offer more.

Unicode contains each character that you can imagine, including extra non-printable ones as well. One of my top choices is the pesky right-to-left mark, which has code point 8207 and is utilized in text with both left-to-right and option to-left language scripts, for example, an article containing both English and Arabic sections.

Unicode versus UTF-8

It didn't take much time for the people to understand that the entirety of the world's characters couldn't be stuffed into one byte each. It's obvious from this that modern, more comprehensive encodings would need to utilize numerous bytes to encode a few characters.

You additionally observed over that Unicode isn't an out and out character encoding. Why would that be?

There is one thing that Unicode doesn't let you know: it doesn't disclose to you how to get actual bits from the text—simply code points. It doesn't reveal to you enough about how to change over text to binary information and the other way around.

Unicode is a technical encoding standard, not an encoding. That is the place UTF-8 and other encoding plans become possibly the most important factor. The Unicode standard (a guide of characters to code focuses) characterizes a few unique encodings from its single character set.

UTF-8, just as its lesser-utilized cousins, UTF-16 and UTF-32, is an encoding format for representing to Unicode characters as binary information of at least one bytes for each character. We'll examine UTF-16 and UTF-32. However, UTF-8 has taken the biggest share of the pie by far.

That carries us to a definition that is long late. I don't get its meaning, officially, to encode and decode?

Python 3: All-In on Unicode

Python 3 has no reservations on Unicode and UTF-8 explicitly. This is what that means:

- Python 3 source code is thought to be UTF-8 as a matter of course. This means you don't require # - *-coding: UTF-8 - *-at the highest point of .py files in Python 3.

- All text (str) is Unicode as a matter of course. Encoded Unicode text is spoken to as parallel information (bytes). The str type can contain any strict Unicode character, for example, "$\Delta v/\Delta t$", which will all be put away as Unicode.

- Python 3 acknowledges numerous Unicode code points in identifiers, which means a list of résumé = "~/Documents/resume.pdf" is substantial if this makes you excited.

- Python's 're' module defaults to there. UNICODE banner instead of re.ASCII. This means, for example, that r"\w" matches Unicode word characters, not simply ASCII letters.

There is one other property that is more nuanced, which is that the default encoding to the implicit open() is platform-dependent and relies upon the benefit of locale.getpreferredencoding():

```
>>> # Mac OS X High Sierra
>>> import locale
>>> locale.getpreferredencoding()
'UTF-8'

>>> # Windows Server 2012; other Windows builds may use UTF-16
>>> import locale
>>> locale.getpreferredencoding()
'cp1252'
```

Once more, the exercise here is to be careful about making assumptions with regards to the all universality of UTF-8, regardless of whether it is the predominant encoding. It never damages to be explicit in your code.

Step by step instructions to Use Generators and yield in Python

Have you at any point needed to work with a dataset so enormous that it overpowered your machine's memory? Or then again, perhaps you have a complex function that requires to keep up an internal state every time it's called, however, the capacity is too little to even think about justifying making its class. In these cases, and the sky is the limit from there, generators and the Python yield statement are here to help.

Utilizing Generators

Presented with PEP 255, generator functions are an uncommon sort of capacity that arrive at a lazy iterator. These are substances that you can loop over like a loop. In any case, in contrast to records, languid iterators don't store their contents in memory. For an outline of iterators in Python, investigate Python "for" Loops (Definite Iteration).

Since you have a harsh thought of what a generator does, you may consider what they resemble in real life. How about taking a look at two examples. In the main, you'll perceive how generators work from a superior view. At that point, you'll zoom in and analyze every model all the more completely.

Model 1: Reading Large Files

A typical instance of using generators is to work with information streams or huge files, as CSV records. These content documents separate information into sections by utilizing commas. This format is a typical method to share information. Now, what if you need to include the number of columns in a CSV file. The code obstruct beneath gives one method of checking those lines:

```
1  csv_gen = csv_reader("some_csv.txt")
2  row_count = 0
3
4  for row in csv_gen:
5      row_count += 1
6
7  print(f"Row count is {row_count}")
8
```

Understanding the Python Yield Statement

In general, the yield is a fairly simple statement. Its essential occupation is to control the flow of a generator function such that it brings explanations back. As quickly referenced above. However, the Python yield statement has a few tricks up its sleeve.

When you call a generator function or utilize a generator expression, you return a unique iterator called a generator. You can dole out this generator to a variable to utilize it. Once you call rare techniques on the generator, for example, next(), the code inside the capacity is executed up to yield.

Once the Python yield statement is hit, the program suspends function execution and returns the yielded value to the caller. (Interestingly, return stops function execution ultimately.) When capacity is suspended, the condition of that capacity is saved. This incorporates any factor ties near the generator, the guidance pointer, the inside stack, and any special case taking care of.

This allows you to continue work execution whenever you call one of the generator's methods. Along these lines, all function evaluation picks back up directly after yield. You can see this in real life by utilizing numerous Python yield statements:

```
>>> def multi_yield():
...     yield_str = "This will print the first string"
...     yield yield_str
...     yield_str = "This will print the second string"
...     yield yield_str
...
>>> multi_obj = multi_yield()
>>> print(next(multi_obj))
This will print the first string
>>> print(next(multi_obj))
This will print the second string
>>> print(next(multi_obj))
Traceback (most recent call last):
  File "<stdin>", line 1, in <module>
StopIteration
```

Utilizing Advanced Generator Methods

You've seen the most widely recognized utilizations and developments of generators, yet there are a couple of more tricks to cover. In addition to yield, generator items can utilize the following methods:

- .send()
- .throw()
- .close()

Step by step instructions to Use.send()

For this next area, you're going to construct a program that utilizes each of the three methods. This program will print numeric palindromes like before, yet with a couple of changes. After experiencing a palindrome, your new program will include a digit and start a quest for the following one from that point. You'll also deal with exceptions with .toss() and stop the generator after a given amount of digits with .close(). To begin with, how about we review

139

the code for your palindrome detector:

```python
1  def is_palindrome(num):
2      # Skip single-digit inputs
3      if num // 10 == 0:
4          return False
5      temp = num
6      reversed_num = 0
7  
8      while temp != 0:
9          reversed_num = (reversed_num * 10) + (temp % 10)
10         temp = temp // 10
11 
12     if num == reversed_num:
13         return True
14     else:
15         return False
16
```

This is a similar code to the one you saw before, then again, actually, now the program carefully returns true or false. You'll also need to adjust your original infinite sequence generator, as so:

```python
1  def infinite_palindromes():
2      num = 0
3      while True:
4          if is_palindrome(num):
5              i = (yield num)
6              if i is not None:
7                  num = i
8          num += 1
9
```

There are a lot of changes here! The first you'll see is in line where i = (yield num). Even though you learned before that yield is a statement, that isn't exactly the entire story.

As of Python 2.5 (a similar release that presented the strategies you are finding out about now), the yield is an expression, instead of a statement. You can, at present use it as a statement. However, presently, you can also utilize it as you find in the code block above, where I take the worth that is yielded. This allows you to control the yielded value. More importantly, it allows you to .send()value back to the generator. Once execution gets after yield, I will take the value that is sent.

You'll also check if I am None, which could occur if next() is approached by the generator object. (This can also happen when you emphasize with a for-loop.) If I have a value, at that point, you update num with the new value. But, whether or not or not I hold value, you'll then increase the num and start the loop again.

Presently, investigate the main function code, which sends the most reduced number with another digit back to the generator. For instance, in case the palindrome is 121, at that point, it will .send() 1000:

```
1  pal_gen = infinite_palindromes()
2  for i in pal_gen:
3      digits = len(str(i))
4      pal_gen.send(10 ** (digits))
5
6
```

With this code, you make the generator object and repeat through it. The program just yields a value once a palindrome is found. It utilizes len() to decide the number of digits in that palindrome. At that point, it sends 10 ** digits to the generator. This brings execution once more into the generator logic and appoints 10 ** digits to I. Since I presently have worth, the program refreshes num, additions, and checks for palindromes again.

When your code finds and yields another palindrome, you'll emphasize using the for-loop. This is equivalent to iterating with next(). The generator also gets up 5 with I = (yield num). In any case, presently I am None since you didn't explicitly send a value.

What you've made here is a coroutine or a generator function into which you can pass information. These are valuable for developing information pipelines, yet as you'll see soon, they aren't vital for building them. (In case you're hoping to jump further, then this seminar on coroutines and concurrency is one of the complete treatments available.)

Since you've found out about .send(), we should investigate .throw().

Step by step instructions to Use .throw()

.throw() allows you to toss exemptions with the generator. In the below model, you raise the special case in line 6. This code will toss a ValueError once digits arrive at 5:

```
1  pal_gen = infinite_palindromes()
2  for i in pal_gen:
3      print(i)
4      digits = len(str(i))
5      if digits == 5:
6          pal_gen.throw(ValueError("We don't like large palindromes"))
7      pal_gen.send(10 ** (digits))
8
```

Step by step instructions to Use .close()

As its name suggests, .close() permits you to stop a generator. This can be particularly handy when controlling a boundless sequence generator. How about we update the code above by evolving .toss() to .close() to stop the iteration:

```python
pal_gen = infinite_palindromes()
for i in pal_gen:
    print(i)
    digits = len(str(i))
    if digits == 5:
        pal_gen.close()
    pal_gen.send(10 ** (digits))
```

Propelled Features of Python and How to Use Them

The propelled features of any programming language are generally found through extensive experience. You're coding up a complicated project and wind up looking for something on StackOverflow. You then run over a beautifully elegant solution for your difficult project that utilizes a Python feature you never at any point knew existed!

That is absolutely the funniest approach to learn: disclosure by investigation and mishap!

Here are 5 of the most valuable propelled highlights of the Python programming language — and even more fundamentally how to use them!

(1) Lambda functions

A Lambda Function is a little, anonymous function — unknown as in it doesn't have a name.

Python functions usually are characterized utilizing the style of def a_function_name(); however, with lambda functions, we don't give it a name by any means. We do this because the motivation behind a lambda function is to play out a simple expression or operation without the requirement for thoroughly characterizing a capacity.

A lambda capacity can take any number of contentions, yet should consistently have just one expression:

```
1  x = lambda a, b : a * b
2  print(x(5, 6)) # prints '30'
3
4  x = lambda a : a*3 + 3
5  print(x(3)) # prints '12'
6
```

Perceive how simple that was! We played out a touch of essential math without the requirement for characterizing an all-out function. This is one of the numerous features of Python that makes it a spotless and simplistic programming language to utilize.

(2) Maps

Map() is a work in Python work used to apply a function to a sequence of components like a list or word reference. It's a perfect and in particular readable manner to perform such an operation.

```
1  def square_it_func(a):
2      return a * a
3
4  x = map(square_it_func, [1, 4, 7])
5  print(x) # prints '[1, 16, 49]'
6
7  def multiplier_func(a, b):
8      return a * b
9
10 x = map(multiplier_func, [1, 4, 7], [2, 5, 8])
11 print(x) # prints '[2, 20, 56]'
12
```

Look at the example above! We can apply our capacity to a single list or various records. Truth be told, you can utilize a map with any python work you can consider, as long as it's perfect with the sequence elements you are operating on.

(3) Filtering

The Filter built-in function is very much like the Map function in that it applies a capacity to a grouping (list, tuple, word reference). The key difference is that filter() will just restore the components which the applied function returned as True.

Look at the model below for an illustration:

```
# Our numbers
numbers = [1, 2, 3, 4, 5, 6, 7, 8, 9, 10, 11, 12, 13, 14, 15]

# Function that filters out all numbers which are odd
def filter_odd_numbers(num):

    if num % 2 == 0:
        return True
    else:
        return False

filtered_numbers = filter(filter_odd_numbers, numbers)

print(filtered_numbers)
# filtered_numbers = [2, 4, 6, 8, 10, 12, 14]
```

In addition to the fact that we evaluated True or False for each list element, the filter() function also made a point just to restore the components which coordinated as True. This is convenient for taking care of two stages of checking an articulation and building an arrival list.

(4) Itertools

The Python Itertools module is an assortment of devices for dealing with iterators. An iterator is an information type that can be utilized in a for-loop, including files, tuples, and word references.

Utilizing the functions in the Itertools module will allow you to perform numerous iterator tasks that would ordinarily require multi-line functions and complicated list comprehension. Look at the models beneath for a great outline of the magic of Itertools!

CHAPTER # 9
COMPARING PYTHON WITH OTHER LANGUAGES

Python is regularly compared with other interpreted languages, for instance, Java, JavaScript, Perl, Tcl, or Smalltalk. Connections with C++, Common Lisp and Scheme can also be enlightening. In this area, I will quickly compare Python with every one of these languages. These comparisons focus on what each language gives as it were. The choice of a programming language is much of the time coordinated by other valid limitations, for example, cost, availability, preparing, and earlier venture, or even emotional attachment. Since these viewpoints are highly variable, it appears to be an exercise in futility to think of them as much for this correlation.

Java

Python programs are commonly expected to run more slowly than Java programs, yet they also set aside substantially less effort to develop. Python programs are ordinarily 3-5 times shorter than identical Java programs. This difference can be credited to Python's worked insignificant level information types and its dynamic composing. For instance, a Python software engineer burns through no time declaring the types of variables or arguments, and Python's powerful polymorphic list. Furthermore, word reference types, for which rich syntactic assistance are joined straight with the language, find use in basically every Python program. Due to the run-time typing, Python's run time must perform more thorough compared to Java programming language. For instance, while evaluating the expression a+b, it should initially investigate the items a and b to find out their type, which isn't known at compile time. It at that point summons the suitable addition operation, which might be an overloaded user-defined method. Java, then again, can play out an effective number or floating-point addition, however, requires variable declarations for a & b, and doesn't allow overloading of the + operator for occurrences of user-defined classes.

Hence, Python is a vastly improved fit as a "glue" language, while Java is better characterized as a low-level utilization language. Honestly, the two together make a brilliant mix. Parts can be created in Java and consolidated to shape applications in Python; Python can also be used to demonstrate fragments until their arrangement can be "hardened" in a Java implementation. To help this sort of progress, a Python implementation written in Java is a work in progress, which allows calling Python code from Java and the opposite way around. In this utilization, Python source code is implied Java bytecode (with help from a run-time library to support Python's dynamic semantics).

JavaScript

Python's "object-based" subset is generally equivalent to JavaScript. Like JavaScript (and not at all like Java), Python supports a programming style that utilizes simple functions and variables without taking part in class definitions. Python, of course, supports writing much bigger projects and better code reuse through a true object-oriented programming style, where classes and inheritance assume a significant role.

Perl

Python and Perl originate from a similar background (UNIX scripting, which both have long outgrown), and sport numerous similar features, yet have an alternate way of functioning. Perl emphasizes support for basic application-oriented tasks, for example, by having worked in regular expressions, file scanning and report creating features. Python emphasizes support for normal programming methodologies, for example, information structure plan and object-oriented programming, and urges software engineers to write readable (and in this way viable) code by giving a rich however not overly cryptic notation. As an outcome, Python approaches Perl yet infrequently beats it in its original application domain; however, Python has relevance well past Perl's speciality.

Tcl

Like Python, Tcl is practical as an app expansion language, as well as an independent programming language. However, Tcl, which generally stores all information as strings, is feeble on information structures and executes common code much slower than Python. Tcl also lacks features required for writing enormous ventures, for instance, specific namespaces. As such, while an "ordinary" enormous application utilizing Tcl ordinarily contains Tcl augmentations inscribed in C or C++ that are clear to that app, an equivalent Python application can frequently be written in "pure Python". Unadulterated Python improvement is a lot faster than to write and debug a C or C++ programming language part. It has been said that Tcl's one saving value is the Tk tool kit. Python has received an interface to Tk as its standard GUI part library.

Tcl 8.0 tends to the speed issues by providing a bytecode compiler with restricted information type backing, furthermore, it incorporates namespaces. Regardless, it is uptil now a fundamentally more cumbersome programming language.

Smalltalk

Maybe the most significant difference among Python and Smalltalk is Python's more "mainstream" syntax, which surrenders it a leg on developer preparing. Like Smalltalk, Python has dynamic and compulsory writing, and everything in Python is an item. However, Python distinguishes worked in object types from user-defined classes and right now doesn't permit inheritance from worked in types. Smalltalk's standard library of assortment information types is increasingly refined, while Python's library has more offices for managing Internet and WWW real factors, for example, email, HTML and FTP.

Python has a different way of functioning concerning the improved condition and distribution of code. Where Smalltalk generally has a monolithic "framework picture" which contains both the earth and the customer's program, Python stores both standard modules and customer modules in singular files which can without much of a stretch be revamped or distributed outside the structure. One result is that there is multiple choice for attaching a Graphical User Interface (GUI) to a Python program since the GUI isn't consolidated with the structure.

C++

Almost all said for Java also applies for C++, simply more so: where Python code is ordinarily 3-5 times shorter than equivalent Java code, it is frequently 5-10 times shorter than equal C++ code! Narrative proof proposes that one Python software engineer can complete in two months what two C++ developers can't finish in a year. Python shimmers as a glue language used to combine components written in C++.

Basic Lisp and Scheme

These languages are near Python in their dynamic semantics, yet so extraordinary in their approach to syntax that a comparison becomes just about a religious argument: is Lisp's lack of syntax a bit of an advantage or a disadvantage? It should be seen that Python has mindful limits like those of Lisp, and Python activities can develop and execute program parts on the fly. Usually, real-world properties are definitive: Common Lisp is large (in each sense), and the Scheme world is divided between numerous incompatible versions, where Python has a single, free, compact implementation.

Significant Reasons Why You Should Use Python language

According to the current TIOBE Programming Community Index, Python is one of the major 10 popular programming languages of 2017. Python is a universally useful and elevated level programming language. You can utilize Python for creating work area GUI applications, sites and web applications. Additionally, Python, as a high-level programming language, allows you to focus on centre usefulness of the application by dealing with regular programming tasks. The basic syntax of the programming language further makes it simpler for you to keep the code base intelligible and application viable.

7 Reasons Why You Must Ruminate Writing Software Applications in Python
1) Clear and Maintainable Code

While coding for an application, you should focus on the nature of its source code to streamline support and updates. The sentence structure rules of Python permit you to communicate ideas without writing extra code. Simultaneously, Python, in comparison to other programming languages, emphasizes code readability and allows you to utilize English keywords rather than punctuation. Subsequently, you can utilize Python to fabricate custom applications without writing extra code. The readable and clean code base will assist you with maintaining and updating the product without investing additional time and energy.

2) Multiple Programming Paradigms

Like other current programming languages, Python also supports a few programming worldviews. It supports object-oriented and organized programming completely. Additionally, its language features help different ideas in functional and aspect-oriented programming. Simultaneously, Python also features a powerful sort framework and programmed memory of the board. The ideal programming models and language of features help you to utilize Python for growing huge and complex programming applications.

3) Compatible with Major Platforms and Systems

At present, Python supports many working frameworks. You can even utilize Python interpreters to run the code on explicit stages and tools. Also, Python is an interpreted programming language. It allows you to run a similar code on different stages without recompilation. Subsequently, you are not required to recompile the code in the wake of making any alteration. You can run the adjusted application code without recompiling and check the effect of changes made to the code right away. The element makes it simpler for you to make changes to the code without increasing development time.

4) Robust Standard Library

Its enormous and robust standard library makes Python score over other programming languages. The standard library allows you to look over a wide scope of modules as per your exact needs. Every module further empowers you to add usefulness to the Python application without writing extra code. For example, while writing a web application in Python, you can utilize explicit modules to actualize web services, perform string activities, manage working framework interface or work with web protocols. You can even assemble data about different modules by browsing through the Python Standard Library documentation.

5) Many Open Source Frameworks and Tools

As an open-source programming language, Python causes you to shorten programming improvement cost significantly. You can even utilize a few open-source Python systems, libraries and development tools to shorten improvement time without increasing development cost. You even have the option to browse a wide scope of open-source Python systems and development tools as per your exact needs. For example, you can improve and speed up web application development by utilizing strong Python web structures like Django, Flask, Pyramid, Bottle and cherrypy. Similarly, you can accelerate desktop GUI application development using Python GUI systems and toolboxs like PyQT, PyJs, PyGUI, Kivy, PyGTK and WxPython.

6) Simplify Complex Software Development

Python is a broadly useful programming language. Consequently, you can utilize the programming language for creating both desktop and web applications. Additionally, you can utilize Python for developing complex scientific and numeric

154

applications. Python is structured with features to facilitate information investigation and perception. You can exploit the information examination features of Python to make big data solution arrangements without investing additional time and energy. Simultaneously, the information perception libraries and APIs given by Python help you to visualize, present and detain an all the more engaging and powerful way. Numerous Python developers even use Python to achieve artificial intelligence (AI) and characteristic language processing tasks.

7) Adopt Test Driven Development

You can utilize Python to make a model of the software application quickly. Also, you can construct the product application directly from the model essentially by refactoring the Python code. Python even makes it more straightforward for you to perform coding and testing all the while by receiving a test driven development (TDD) approach. You can easily write the necessary tests before writing code and utilize the tests to evaluate the application code continuously. The tests can also be utilized for checking if the application meets predefined requirements dependent on its source code.

However, Python, like other programming languages, has its weaknesses. It comes up short on a portion of the built-in features given by another present-day programming language. Subsequently, you need to utilize Python libraries, modules, and structures to accelerate custom software development. Also, a few examinations have indicated that Python is slower than a few generally utilized programming languages, including Java and C++. You need to accelerate the Python application by making changes to the application code or utilizing custom runtime. However, you can generally go through Python to speed software development and simplify software maintenance.

Advantages and Disadvantages of Python Programming Language

Python is an elevated level, interpreted and universally useful powerful programming language that centres on code readability. The language structure in Python encourages the programmers to do coding in fewer steps when contrasted with Java or C++. The language established in the year 1991 by the developer Guido Van Rossum makes the programming simple and fun to do. The Python is broadly utilized in greater associations given its numerous programming ideal models. They usually include goal and article situated useful programming. It has a complete and huge standard library that has programmed memory management and dynamic features.

Why Companies Prefer Python?

Python has topped the statistics in recent years over other programming languages like C, C++ and Java and is commonly used by the programmers. The language has experienced an exceptional change, since its discharge 25 years back, to the same number of add-on highpoints which are accessible. The Python 1.0 had the module arrangement of Modula-3 and associated with Amoeba Operating System with shifted functioning instruments. Python 2.0 introduced in the year 2000 had features of the garbage collector and Unicode. Python 3.0, introduced in the year 2008, had a constructive design that avoids copy modules and builds. With the additional features, presently, the organizations are utilizing Python 3.5.

The software development companies incline toward Python language as a result of its adaptable features and less programming codes. About 14% of the programmers use it on the working frameworks like UNIX, Linux, Windows and Mac OS. The software engineers of enormous organizations use Python as it has made a mark for itself in the product advancement with characteristic features like-

- Interactive
- Interpreted
- Modular
- Dynamic
- Object-oriented
- Portable
- High level
- Extensible in C++ & C

Advantages of Python

The Python language has expanded application in the product advancement organizations, for example, in gaming, web systems and applications, language advancement, prototyping, visual communication applications, and so on. This gives the language a higher rating over other programming languages utilized in the business. A portion of its advantages are:

- **Extensive Support Libraries**

It has enormous standard libraries that incorporate areas like string tasks, Internet, web service instruments, working framework interfaces and protocols. The greater part of the highly used programming tasks is now scripted into it which restricts the length of the codes to be written in Python.

- **Integration Feature**

Python coordinates the Enterprise Application Integration that makes it simple to create Web benefits by summoning COM or COBRA components. It has amazing control abilities as it calls directly through C, C++ or Java using Python. Python also forms XML and other markup languages as it can run on all cutting edge working frameworks through same byte code.

- **Improved Programmer's Productivity**

The language has extensive help libraries and clean object-oriented designs that expand two to ten times of programmer's productivity while utilizing the languages like Java, VB, Perl, C, C++ and C#.

- **Productivity**

With its solid procedure, mix highlights, unit testing system and upgraded control abilities contribute towards the speeding up for most applications and efficiency of uses. It is an incredible alternative for building versatile multi-protocol network applications.

Restrictions or Disadvantages of Python

Python has varied advantageous features, and developers lean toward this language compared to other programming languages since it is anything but difficult to learn and code as well. Notwithstanding, this language has still not made its place in some figuring fields that incorporate Enterprise Development Shops. Along these lines, this language may not understand a portion of the enterprise solutions, and limitations included.

- **Difficulty in Using Other Languages**

The Python sweethearts become so familiar with its features and its extensive libraries, so they face issues in learning or dealing with other programming languages. Python specialists may see the proclaiming of cast "qualities" or variable "types", syntactic requirements of including wavy supports or semicolons as a difficult assignment.

- **Weak in Mobile Computing**

Python has made its quality on numerous work area and server stages, however it is viewed as a weak language for mobile computing. This is the explanation as to why not many mobile applications are worked in it like Carbonnelle.

- **Gets Slow**

Python executes with the assistance of an interpreter rather than the compiler, which makes it delayed because compilation and execution help it to work regularly. Then again, it tends to be seen to run quick for some web applications as well.

- **Run-time Errors**

The Python language is more composed, so it has many structure limitations that are reported by some Python developers. It is even observed that it requires more testing time, and the mistakes show up when the applications are finally run.

- **Underdeveloped Database Access Layers**

When compared with the well-known technologies like JDBC and ODBC, Python's database in getting to layer is seen as a bit underdeveloped and primitive. However, it can't be applied in the undertakings that need a smooth connection of complex legacy information.

World-Class Software Companies That Use Python

There are more than 500 current programming languages, with more being written each day. Truly, most of these overlap and a huge number were never intended to be utilized outside a casual or lab setting. However, for the programming languages that are utilized in regular coding and organizations, you need to settle on a decision. What languages would it be a good idea for you to learn, and can it be easy for you to place your time in learning them?

As this is a site dedicated to Python, we've just revealed to you why Python is an extraordinary language to learn. Also, you likely think about how Python is presumably the most favoured language for the Raspberry Pi (as most come preloaded with it). Also, realizing that you recognize what amazing things you can do with a Pi unit and only a little ingenuity. While it's not hard to see how you can fiddle with Python, you may be thinking about how this means real business and real-world applications.

What we will do now is educate you concerning eight leading organizations using it so that you realize the utilization Python. That way, you can perceive what extraordinary real-world opportunities there are for Python developers out there.

Modern Light and Magic

Modern Light and Magic (MLM) is the special effects powerhouse that set up different blockbuster movies. Both now and in the foreseeable future, they've gotten synonymous with FX, winning numerous awards for their work in movies and commercials. In their initial days, MLM focused on functional impacts, however they before long understood that PC created impacts were the future of FX as a rule.

Initially, MLM's CGI studio ran off of a UNIX shell, yet this was just dealing with a generally low measure of work. Since the studio predicted the future of CGI, they began searching for a framework that could deal with the aggressive upscaling that they discovered later on. MLM chose Python 1.4 over Perl and Tcl, choosing to use Python since it was much faster to incorporate into their current infrastructure. Due to Python's simple interoperability with C and C++, it was basic for MLM to bring Python into their exclusive lighting programming. This allows them to maintain the python in different places, utilizing it for wrapping programming components and broadening their standard graphics applications.

The studio has utilized Python in various highlights of their work. Specialists use Python to track and audit pipeline functionality, keeping up a database of each picture delivered for each film. As more and more of MLM's projects were controlled by Python, it made a simpler unified toolset that took into account a more effective creation pipeline. For a real model, look no farther than OpenEXR, an HD document group used by MLM. As a part of the pack, PyIlmBase is included (even though it has a Boost reliance).

Regardless of various reviews, MLM keeps on seeing Python as the best answer for its needs. The combination of an open-source code joined with the capacity to back-port changes guarantees that Python will keep on addressing MLM's necessities for a long period.

Google

Google has been a follower of Python from almost the earliest reference point. In the first place, the founders of Google settled on the choice of "Python where we can, C++ where we should." This meant C++ was utilized where memory control was the goal, and low latency was wanted. In different aspects, Python enabled for simplicity of maintenance and relatively fast delivery.

In any event, when different scripts were written for Google in Perl or Bash, these were frequently recorded into Python. The explanation was a direct result of the simplicity of sending and how simple Python is to keep up. Indeed, as indicated by Steven Levy – writer of "In the Plex," Google's absolute first web-crawling spider was first written in Java 1.0 and was difficult to such an extent that they changed it into Python.

Facebook

Facebook production engineers are exceptionally keen about Python, making it the third most mainstream language at the online life goliath (simply behind C++ and their proprietary PHP tongue, Hack). All around, there are more than 5,000 spotlights on utilities and services at Facebook, managing framework, paired dispersion, hardware imaging, and operational automation.

The simplicity of utilizing Python libraries means that the creation engineers don't need to compose or keep up as much code, allowing them to focus on getting upgrades live. It also guarantees that the foundation of Facebook can scale proficiently.

Python is right now answerable for numerous services in framework management. These incorporate utilizing TORconfig to deal with organize switch setup and imaging, FBOSS for white box switch CLIs, and utilizing Dapper for booking and execution of maintenance work.

Facebook has distributed various open-source Python projects written for Py3, including a Facebook Ads API and a Python Async IRCbot system. Facebook is at present updating their foundation or, handlers to 3.4 from 2, and AsyncIO is helping their designers all the while.

Instagram

In 2016, the Instagram designing group flaunted that they were running the world's most prominent arrangement of the Django web system, which is written entirely in Python. This remains constant today.

From that point forward, Instagram's building group has put time and assets into keeping their Python sending feasible at the enormous scale (~800 million month to month dynamic clients) they're working at:

"With the work we've placed into building the effectiveness

system for Instagram's web service, we are certain that we will continue scaling our service structure using Python. We've in like manner started to place more into the Python language itself, and are beginning to examine moving our Python from version 2 to 3."

In 2017, Instagram relocated the greater part of their Python code base from Python 2.7 to Python 3. You can watch the PyCon 2017 keynote talk that Lisa Guo and Hui Ding gave and find out about their involvement in this huge code migration.

CONCLUSION

Python is an item arranged, high-level programming language with unique incorporated semantics principally for web and application development. It is amazingly attractive in the field of Rapid Application Development since it offers dynamic typing and dynamic binding options. Python is generally easy, so it's anything but difficult to learn since it requires a particular language structure that focuses on readability. Developers can read and interpret Python code a lot simpler than different programming languages. Thus, this decreases the expense of program maintenance and development because it allows groups to work cooperatively without critical language and experience barriers. The possibility of a "scripting language" has changed widely since its inception, as Python is presently used to write enormous, business style applications, rather than simply common ones. This dependence on Python has become considerably more so as the internet gained popularity. A vast larger part of web applications and stages depend on Python, including Google's web crawler, YouTube, and the web-arranged exchange arrangement of the New York Stock Exchange (NYSE). You should understand that the language must be really certifiable when it's controlling a stock exchange system.

Moreover, Python reinforces the use of modules and packages, which means that activities can be organized in a specific style, and code can be reused over a variety of projects. When you've built up a module or package you need, it very well may be scaled for use in various exercises, and it's not hard to import or incorporate these modules. One of the most reassuring focal points of Python is that both the standard library and the translator are accessible for nothing out of your pocket, in both parallel and source structure. There is no selectiveness either, as Python and all the important devices are available on every significant stage. Along these lines, it is an enticing choice for developers who would prefer not to stress over paying high improvement prices.

If this depiction of Python is over your head, don't stress. You'll understand it soon enough. What you have to take away from this is that Python is a programming language used to make programming on the web and in application structure, including mobile. It's generally simple to learn, and the important tools are available to all for nothing out of pocket.

You can perceive that it is so easy to write anything with Python. I trust you currently have a good concept of what Python is. The features it has and how you can utilize it for nearly anything that you need to code and to summarize everything, the professions that you seek after are on a consistent rise and are rewarding.

www.ingramcontent.com/pod-product-compliance
Lightning Source LLC
Chambersburg PA
CBHW052354220526
45465CB00003BA/1108